SOME MISTAKES ARE
GREAT KISSERS

With love and Abundance,

SOME MISTAKES ARE
GREAT KISSERS
A Dating Memoir

DR. STEFANIE KLEINE &
ERIN MORONI

Some Mistakes are Great Kissers
© 2020 Dr. Stefanie Kleine

Beloved Rebel Media
http://www.belovedrebelmedia.com

ISBN: 978-1-7342905-7-8

The events described within this compilation are the author's personal thoughts and recollections. The dialogue is written to the best of the author's recount of the events that took place.

Book Cover Illustration & Design by Heidi Dorey
Cover Photograph by Aeron McKeough
Interior Design by Danielle H. Acee

Printed in the United States of America

To my Mom and Dad...
for showing me just how deeply I deserve to be loved.

"One day someone will walk into your life and make you see why it never worked out with anyone else." (Proverb)

Table of Contents

Stefanie Acknowledgments

God & Universe – For all the blessings and for being with me every step of the way. You are my compass.

Mom & Dad – I am so blessed to do life with you. You have always made sure that I knew my worth. Thank you for raising me to be independent, loving, and strong. Next time around, would you mind also teaching me that bit about men wanting to feel needed? I had to learn that one the hard way. "Thank you" will never even come close to being enough. You have given me everything. I love you past infinity.

Bub – For having my back and for showing me what it feels like to be deeply adored and loved. I know this book was difficult to witness. Thank you for hanging in there, for all of your creative suggestions, and for keeping me heavily caffeinated. Our relationship is what gave me the hutzpah to finally write this book. You are my best friend…in this life and the 600 years that came before it. I love you, Bia.

My Favorite Girls (Jana, Carol, Cami, Pitter, Jen, Becky, Aunt Shari, Aunt Jan, Giedre, Jess, Debra, and Erica) – for laughing, crying, and being readily available to drink far too much wine with me as I made my way through the land of Bobs. Ladies, we have countless memories and you are always in my heart. This life has so much more meaning because you are in it.

My Favorite Boys (Reggie, Augustine, Robert, Jay, Simone, Josh, and Uncle Avery) – for continually reminding me that I am special, deserving, "top shelf" and "high fruit."

Dr. Deborah and Dr. Shelly Kleine – for being the two most influential professors of my life. For recognizing my gifts and always championing my spirit. Shelly, I know you are watching over me. I wish you could have met Bub so you could have asked him your favorite question, "Do you have what it takes to be with a woman who is both beautiful and brilliant?" I am certain you would have been very pleased with his response.

Magie – for being one of my dearest friends and one of the most spectacular human beings I have ever known. I know you are in Heaven, radiating beauty, and rocking the most glamorous pair of angel wings. Thank you for helping me believe that I would make it through to "the other side of heartache."

Veronica, Kathy, Leora, Molly, and Wendy – for your genuine encouragement through this incredibly vulnerable process. Your belief in me was often the fuel that kept me pressing on through the long hours, deep excavations, and scary moments. When I would have doubts and question why anyone would want to hear my story, I would hear you ladies in my head. Without this, I am not sure I would have persevered in sharing such personal details about my life.

Mama C – for teaching me the 3 P's when it comes to men.

Shanda – for snapping me out of even thinking about ever being in victim consciousness. And for turning me on to Wayne Dyer so many years ago. Both of these things have fundamentally changed my life.

Aeron – for your talent and patience while shooting the cover. And for always checking in with me about the status of my book. Those gentle nudges came to mind in the moments I wanted to hide and call it quits.

Danielle Cohen Joseph - for making yourself available to me in the earliest stages of this journey.

Darryl Cohen – for teaching Erin and I how to CYA.

Sara Kocek – for being an incredible source of reassurance and guidance. And for being a damn good editor.

Danielle Acee – for holding our hand through this process. You made it all feel so possible.

Erin Moroni – for being my Rumpelstiltskin, one my very best friends, and the reason I was able to actually make this happen. You have set the bar so unbelievably high as a partner that I am pretty certain I will never be able to work with anyone else. Smart move, sister. I cherish you. We do brave things, so…here we go!

Erin Acknowledgments

I would like to express my sincere thanks to the following people: Mike, you are my favorite husband in the whole world. Thank you for giving me the space and grace to complete this calling. I cannot rightfully express the depths of my gratitude for the life you have afforded us. Thank you for letting me turn our closet into my office for the better part of a year, for being my IT guy throughout this process, and for being such a wonderful father to our girls. I love you. So much.

To G, B, and A, thank you for picking me to be your mom/step-mom. I have loved each of you unconditionally since the first time I laid eyes on you. Thank you for being my greatest teachers and my most cherished gifts. Watching you grow into the powerful, brilliant, capable, creative, interesting, driven, kind, beautiful human beings that you are, has undoubtedly been the greatest privilege of my life. The world became infinitely better when you arrived. I love you forever and ever.

Mom, thank you for being my greatest role model. You have remained steadfast with your faith in me, even when I struggled to see my own worth. You are the most humble, gracious warrior I have ever encountered. Your strength, brilliance, hilarity, and grace never cease to amaze me. I am eternally grateful to have been raised by one of the effervescent souls to walk this earth. I love you, Mama.

Erika, how incredibly lucky am I that my best friend also happens to be my sister? Thank you for being the brilliant, powerful, beautiful, breathtaking, being of light that you are. Thank you for reminding me to be brave and for holding out your hand to steady me when I stumble. You are my closest confidant and my safest place in a world that frequently overwhelms me. I am so proud of you. I love you always.

Sara and Danielle, thank you for your tireless work in editing and formatting this book. You are my she-roes.

Dad, Kathy, Poppy Doodles, Aunt Lisa, Aves, Michael, Doug, Mer, Chad and Jen L., and my precious readers of Erin-Says.com, thank you for always cheering me on. I cannot rightfully express how much more fun this life is with you in it. I love you all.

Stefanie, thank you from the bottom of my heart for this incredible opportunity. Thank you for trusting me with your story. Thank you for your diligence and equally for your patience. It was the greatest of honors to work with you. I truly could not have asked for a better partner. I will treasure this memory forever. I am so excited for all that is and all that is to come. I love you, precious friend.

Foreword

first met Stefanie when she crashed my Christmas party a couple years ago. She ended up partaking in our wholesome family tradition of drinking wine and playing *Cards Against Humanity* much as everyone does on religious holidays. Stefanie informed us she was Jewish so it really didn't matter anyway. I just nodded. Solid point.

Our paths crossed again a year later, when I randomly saw a post Stefanie had made on Facebook seeking a "writer" for a book she wanted written. For some unknown reason, I instinctively knew that post was intended for me. I also knew I wasn't going to respond. Although the idea of writing a book was admittedly an exciting prospect, it seemed utterly monumental and terrifying. Besides, I was content writing my blog that I had started years ago. I was busy raising three children, being a dentist's wife, adopting dogs, going to the mall, volunteering, and researching surgical procedures that could make me prettier. I didn't have time for such frivolous matters, so I quickly put the fantasy out of my mind.

The next day, I received a call from an unknown number. I had a gut feeling it was Stefanie. No, I do not know why I chose to answer. Without even saying hello, she quickly rattled off in her exuberant and bubbly voice, "Soooooo did you see my post about writing a book? That was for you, silly! Why didn't you respond? What day can you meet? Is Thursday good? I will just come to your house since I already know where you live! Eeeee! I am SO excited!"

Jesus Christ. Okay. What drugs is this chick on? *So* she was coming over. Fine. I would simply tell her that I could *not* write her book then. Whatever Sister. Little did I know what was about to hit me. Or more like bitch slap me.

True to her word, Stefanie came over and confidently strode on in. I watched in bewildered amusement as she screamed in terror over my two giant German Shepherds, hugged my kids, and then beelined over to peruse my wine collection until she found a bottle she deemed acceptable. We made our way downstairs into the spare bedroom that I had lovingly deemed "my office" for the evening.

My eyes nervously darted back and forth as she plopped down into a chair and immediately launched into how she wanted to write a book about her life, specifically about the men she had dated and the relationships she had been in. I politely interjected that I wasn't sure I was the right person for the job. Stefanie just stared at me, laughed and said, "Of COURSE you are!"

Meanwhile, I sat there thinking, "What is her deal? She doesn't even know me, and this is literally insane. But I'll humor her." So I took a deep breath and pulled out what would eventually be the first of many, many, maaaany yellow legal pads to start taking notes.

Stefanie began to tell me about one of the men she had recently been on a date with. I listened and took scrupulous notes. By the time she was finished telling me this particular story, I had snot and tears pouring down my face from laughing. Interesting. Maybe I could write for her ass after all. This girl was actually funny. Three hours went by before I finally told her I would write one chapter and see if this was what she was looking for. A week later, I sent over her first chapter and thus began our nine-month journey together as we created this book...her book.

Stefanie and I had infinite lengthy conversations. We had "sleepovers" where we would stay up all night drinking coffee, laughing, crying and raging as she would recount stories of her life. I took diligent notes, even in our sleep-deprived delirium, returned home and promptly began writing up her story. Together, Stefanie and I would go back and forth making change after change, until we were satisfied with each chapter before steadfastly moving onto the next one.

Meanwhile, I was simultaneously juggling my household and my own blog. I finally resorted to writing in my closet because this was seemingly the only place that offered me some form of solace so I could focus. On one particularly challenging day, I felt doubt begin to surface. I was entirely overwhelmed by everybody requiring my attention.

I happened to glance up from the floor in my closet through my tears of frustration and noticed the "manifestation jar" that my daughter had made for me sitting on a shelf. Over the years, I had written on the tiny slips of paper and stuck them in there. I grabbed it and emptied it on the floor of my closet. I unfolded a piece of paper and in my handwriting read the words: "Write a book." I suddenly started laughing. Of course, I had unknowingly manifested this opportunity.

It's funny how the Universe works. One day a Jewish chick is crashing your Christmas party and the next thing you know, she has entrusted you to write some of her deepest, darkest secrets. I sat and silently acknowledged Stefanie's willingness to lean in and be vulnerable. I held space for the tremendous amount of courage this required on her part to share not just the funny life experiences, but also the ones that have evoked great sorrow, embarrassment, shame, love and loss. I was also filled with an immense sense of humility and gratitude, knowing that Stefanie had somehow deemed me, a stranger, worthy of writing her story.

I admittedly had no idea that writing Stefanie's book would serve as a catalyst of great change in my own life. While I was entirely out of my comfort zone, I was also determined to embrace this opportunity. Even though I was long removed from the dating scene, so much of what Stefanie said deeply resonated with me. How many times had I made myself appear smaller or pretended to be happy to satiate those around me? How many times had I apologized for things I was not sorry for to maintain peace? What if it was possible to have a family and a career? What if this was part of the plan all along? Did I really want to spend my remaining time on earth scared to take any risks? And what if it was actually empowering my children to pursue their unique passions by utilizing my God-given talents? Isn't that what I want for them?

What began as writing a light-hearted, funny book evolved into something so much greater. The very process of putting Stefanie's words to paper challenged every belief system I had so eloquently placed in the neatly organized categories of my mind. Maybe there wasn't right or wrong, good or bad, light or dark after all. In fact, maybe every experience I had ever had was entirely necessary for my evolution as a person and an author. Writing her story summoned all the feels, from euphoric laughter to paralyzing pain and every emotion in between. I can surmise your experiences will be somewhat similar as you embark on a brief interlude of Stefanie's earth journey. I mean, the girl definitely gets herself into some weird shit. It is seriously SO awesome.

More than anything, I learned that I needn't ever concern myself with the "how" something will be accomplished. I simply need to keep the vision and have the unwavering faith that everything is going according to plan. Time and again, obstacles would present themselves to us, but even in the face of adversity, we would always find a solution. When one of us would grow weary, the other would pick up the baton and run. Stefanie and I did this time and again, allowing the ebb and flow of creation to work though us. Until finally, we achieved our goal. It was an almost ethereal experience to be part of a team where we both felt fully supported, deeply loved, and utterly determined to complete what we had set out to accomplish.

There is little doubt in my mind that everyone who reads this book will benefit in some way. Stefanie has a unique gift of leaving a lasting impact on everyone she meets. I sincerely hope her story brings you great laughter, a brief escape, deep contemplation of your own relationships, and the ultimate reminder to be gentle on yourself. We are all here to learn from every person and every situation.

In the meantime, I will be basking in the solitude of my newly rented office since I adamantly refuse to write another solitary sentence from the confines of my closet.

Much Love,
Erin

Introduction

"**S**tef, if you hit 50mph on this radar gun, Mom and I will buy you a trampoline."

At the ripe old age of ten, this was music to my ears. I pitched that softball until my arm practically fell off. But you know what? I got my damn trampoline. (I also got tendinitis by the time I turned fifteen, but whatever.)

I grew up playing catch with my dad every single day. Every. Single. Day. Over and over I would pitch the softball to him. My dad was my coach and my greatest champion. From about eight years old, the plan was for me to get a full-ride scholarship and to one day play in the Olympic Games. My dad pushed me hard and celebrated me even harder. The image of his massive stature sitting on an old white paint bucket, catching balls is still permanently etched into my heart. From a very young age, I knew three things about men: they are devoted; they want you to succeed; and the more you succeed—the more they love you.

The discussion around our dinner table was always one of two things: softball or how to run a successful business. I took this shit seriously. When I was eight years old, I crushed it on "business

1

day" at school. I can't remember exactly what I did to win, but it is not out of the realm of possibilities that I ran a successful Ponzi scheme for the day.

I quickly figured out that the harder I worked and the greater my accomplishments, the more I was admired. I earned perfect grades. I was featured in local newspapers for my softball victories. I trained for a scholarship and was an Olympic hopeful. I am a life-long member of MENSA. I earned my Doctorate in Psychology. I coached top corporations and even became a successful real estate investor. I acted in movies and did a handful of modeling gigs. I did everything I could to ensure I was the strong, independent, successful woman that my parents had diligently shaped me to become.

As I grew older, it seemed only natural for me to apply this programming to my relationships. But it was a painful lesson when I discovered that the same rules governing my childhood didn't necessarily apply to my love life. Not everyone celebrated my achievements. Not everyone embraced my successes. And most certainly, not everyone was there to "catch" me.

Men would come on strong, often shower me with extravagant gifts, display signs of adoration and even infatuation, but then they would inexplicably become competitive, or jealous, and some would simply just leave without warning. Time after time, men would tell me they "weren't worthy" or that I was "out of their league." I slowly began hiding my accomplishments and downplaying my achievements. I rationalized that if I made myself appear smaller men would somehow feel less intimidated.

Throughout my life, I had always been able to accomplish everything I put my mind to. And yet, the one thing I wanted more than anything was also the one thing that eluded me time and again…I wanted to meet my person. I deeply desired to have someone to share my life with, to raise a family with, to grow old and move to Florida and die with. I never dreamed I would be unmarried at forty with a batch of genetically superior eggs (I am an Ashkenazi Jew, our DNA goes for top dollar) now frozen and safely stored at a reproductive center.

Alas, here I am.

But it was not due to a lack of effort. I fucking refused to start adopting cats and wearing a mood ring. Instead, I made dating a full-time job. I was determined to find my perfect partner. I went on so many dates that my family and friends started to refer to these men as "Bobs" because it was too hard to remember all their names. I had my dating uniforms—the same outfits for every first and second and third date. I shaved my legs and meticulously maintained my lady garden. I was in it to win it.

Meeting men was easy; finding one that wasn't a total freakshow was not. I went out with a man from Africa only to learn he was already in an arranged marriage. I went out with another guy who was 5'2, with braces, who ditched *me* at a restaurant. I went out with a cop who ended up being a total stalker and jerked off on my front door. Another dude spent our entire two-hour date talking about his ex-wife. I went out with a man who owned a bunch of pit bulls and graciously offered to inseminate me since "we aren't getting any younger." Thank God that at least some of these mistakes were great kissers.

With the persistent urging of my friends, I decided to write a book about some of the crazy shit that has happened on my quest to find true love. Some of these stories are hilarious, some are painful, and some are just plain bizarre-o. I wanted to shine a light on the beautiful and the tragic when it comes to finding love. I also want you to know you are not alone, that we ALL go through things.

Rumor has it that none of us are getting out of here alive, so we might as well come sliding into the proverbial afterlife with our knee pads ripped to shreds, a raspberry on our ass, and the satisfaction of knowing we played a good game.

Love,
Stef

PS. I changed some names to protect the guilty, but everything else is true.

*Including the part about me being an escort.

Devirginator Bob

Growing up, my parents would often take me and my friends to Lake Havasu on the weekends. Conveniently, this is where I met my first "real" boyfriend when I was fifteen. My innocent mom lovingly still refers to him as "that homeless boy." Devirginator Bob was seventeen, super cute, and couch-surfing at friends' houses since his home life was tumultuous.

After seeing Bob on two separate weekends, we shared our first kiss. I remember being so nervous about our date that night, I couldn't even eat. This may not seem like a big deal to some of you, but I am Jewish, so food addiction is genetically encoded in me. Anyway, I had never kissed a boy and had zero clue what I was doing. Fortunately, my older sister had lots of experience and taught me the basics. Before you get weirded out, calm down, she taught me on her hand. I will always remember getting ready for my very first date as my sister and I took turns making out on her hand.

Growing up, I was such a prude that the thought of kissing a boy was terrifying. I used to strategically excuse myself to the bathroom during junior high school parties when the cool kids wanted to play spin the bottle. I'd stay in there as long as I possibly could. And when I had to reluctantly get out, usually because someone else had to pee, I would return to the circle only to will that damn bottle with all my might to NOT land on me.

So you can imagine that when my first kiss was incredibly idyllic, standing barefoot on the beach at sunset, I was positively elated. It was something out of a dream. And I will admit, making out came naturally. Thanks for the pointers, sis!

Devirginator Bob was my first experience with a boy, and I fell hard. Some call it puppy love, but all I know is my knees were wobbly, butterflies had permanently moved into my tummy, and I was completely distracted from everything but Bob. When it was time to head back to California, I was devastated to leave him. Life at fifteen didn't feel right without Bob. I knew I had to find a way to rectify this situation.

Approaching the situation as though Bob was a stray dog, I secretly asked my mom if "we could keep him." I made sure my dad did not overhear my plea because that would have been a hard no. Knowing my mom was a total softie, I was confident I could win her over. And because my mom can talk her way into anything, once I had her vote, I was certain she would be able to convince my dad. Of course, neither of my parents had any idea that Bob and I were an item when I pleaded my heartfelt case. They reluctantly agreed to let Bob live with us. And just like that, we took him home. Not. Fucking. Kidding.

My parents became Bob's guardians, he went to work for them at one of their stores, and they helped him get enrolled in high school. Meanwhile, I gave my virginity to Bob. After three months, my incredibly astute mom figured out that Bob and I were more than just friends and surmised it would be best to secretly rent him an apartment and a car so my dad wouldn't lose his mind. My mom is my ride or die; the woman is a true homie.

To this day, my dad has no idea what really goes on. My mom and I just give him the watered down, edited version of everything because he is prone to outbursts. He totally loses his shit over minor things like moving a dude into his house that his teenage daughter is sleeping with. It can be super annoying, but we have learned to adapt.

Anyway, at first this little arrangement was a dream cometh true. I had never had a boyfriend before so I really liked how Bob would endlessly dote on me. He would walk me to class, carry my books, and meet up with me afterwards. If we weren't together, he was paging me. Hello 90's! For the first time ever, I felt desirable. I went from awkward tomboy to the envy of all the girls in high school.

To say that my mom and dad are chronic worriers with helicopter-parent tendencies would be the understatement of my life. Safety was of utmost importance in our home and we religiously checked in with each other when we stayed overnight elsewhere, traveled, or were simply out of each other's sight for more than a couple hours. So it felt natural to be with a boy who was also incredibly concerned with my whereabouts. Bob would freak out if I was even two minutes late to meet him somewhere or if I didn't immediately return his calls. I figured he was just being chivalrous with his actions because I had learned at a young age to equate love with worry. I didn't understand what was really going on—that Bob was totally possessive over me.

Bob began to "punish" me for my behavior infractions by giving me the silent treatment or interrogating me to the point of absurdity. Bob constantly accused me of cheating on him and would demand to know where I was. Part of me, my ego, was flattered that someone cared that much about me. The other part of me, the sane part, was uncomfortable with what was happening, but I didn't have enough experience to know that it was wrong. I justified his outrageous behavior by telling myself that this is how he showed love.

Though I didn't tell anyone about the outbursts, my friends began to notice and expressed their concerns by pointing out that Bob was jealous and controlling. I began to rebel more and more against Bob's rules by not always immediately returning his calls or even refusing to tell him where I was. As I sought to reclaim my independence, Bob became more intense in his responses.

Everything came to a head one day when I went over to his apartment. Bob and I began arguing and he grabbed my wrists, pushed me against the door, and refused to let me leave. No one had ever put their hands on me in anger before, and I was absolutely terrified. I waited until he calmed down a bit and bolted out of the apartment.

That was the last time I ever saw Bob. He repeatedly called my parents' house sobbing uncontrollably. That weekend, I left for Lake Havasu with my family. When we returned, Bob was gone.

I now realize I confused Bob's possessiveness and controlling behavior with love. My parents often showed their love through protection. So, it only made sense that I had this association. The difference is that my parents did it from a place of really caring for my well-being; Bob did it from a place of insecurity, driven by his own childhood abandonment issues. I used to believe that abuse only happened in Lifetime movies or inside of broken homes with the kind of people you see on Jerry Springer. The truth is, he was physically aggressive and emotionally abusive with me and I was from a beautiful family, a wealthy town, and had solid self-esteem (for a fifteen year old).

Devirginator Bob—not my person.

Take It From Me...
- Silent Treatment is abuse.
- Do not confuse possessiveness with love.
- Abusive relationships can happen at any age and to anyone.
- Always heed to your intuition; if something feels wrong, it is.
- Big sisters are the best make-out teachers.

Cheetah Bob

As a teenager growing up in Southern California, I was always at Knott's Berry Farm with my friends. I was sixteen and had just ditched Devirginator Bob, my first of what would be many, many, many boyfriends. Oh relax, eye roll. I didn't have sex with all of them. Like definitely some of them, but I am not even sure the micro-penis and the erectile dysfunction one counted. Anyway…

My friends and I started chatting up a couple of boys named Avi and Cheetah Bob at the log ride (no pun, although one of these dudes eventually did fall in the log penetration category.) Cheetah Bob was super good-looking. Like, straight up gooorgeous. We all went to a hypnotist show together, where the boys were randomly picked out of the crowd to go on stage. Bob looked sexy as hell, even under a trance clucking like a chicken all over the stage.

Bob didn't really pay any attention to me. However, Avi proceeded to tell me he had a girlfriend and then totally tried to kiss me. I obviously declined his advances, but ended up giving him my pager number. Yes. PAGER number. That is indicative of just how long I have been at this game.

Avi and I stayed in touch, and he invited me to a party a couple weeks later, where I ran into Cheetah Bob again. This time it was game on. We became boyfriend and girlfriend, and people—some of them complete strangers—started referring to us as Ken and Barbie. So much so, that a company considered hiring us to dress up and go their kids' birthday parties.

Bob was two years older, and had gone to school with the band "No Doubt" before they hit the big time. At sixteen, having a hot boyfriend from the other side of town was extra fun. We went to house parties, the beach, concerts, and to the Men's World Cup. Bob even helped my parents plan my 17th birthday party where they surprised me with a limo for the night. Bob came from a close family and his mom was French. (In hindsight, this should have been my first red flag.)

My dad was strict, but my mom convinced him to let Cheetah Bob stay the night, as long as he slept on the floor. So of course, it was way more fun to spend the night at Bob's family's house because his parents actually let us sleep in the same bed. It was seriously so awesome, even though it's not like we knew any fancy, advanced tongue tricks at that point. We were just your basic missionary style young lovers. I imagine this is how young Mormons are when they first get married. But it totes got the job done.

Bob worked for a friend's welding company and had to go to Las Vegas with his boss and some of the other guys he worked with. He was supposed to be home the day before Valentine's Day, and since my parents were going to be out of town, I decided I was going to throw a "couples" house party. Bob assured me he would be back in time.

On Valentine's Day, I went out of my way to look super hot, circa 1997 style, with my baby doll dress and Doc Martens. All my friends and their boyfriends arrived and everyone beelined to the jacuzzi and pool in the backyard while I patiently waited for Bob. I tried to page him. Nothing. The fucker didn't show up. So basically, I threw a romantic party for my friends. I was fuming.

When Bob eventually did get home, I was rip-roaring pissed. Something felt off and I was onto him. Bob eventually came clean (I use this term loosely, keep reading) and admitted to cheating on me with a stripper from Cheetah's. He told me that he was pressured by all the older guys he worked with. All I heard was: A. Mother. Fucking. Stripper. In. Vegas.

Bob was super remorseful, but I did not give him the option of staying together. I was done. Barbie and Ken broke up because Ken couldn't keep his wonder worm in his pants. I did contemplate making solo appearances at birthday parties as "newly single, doesn't-need-a-man, confident, Barbie who doesn't take any shit from her stripper cheating boyfriend." I like to think my new role would have been much more influential and empowering to these little girls.

I eventually forgave him and Bob and I remained friends for many years after he completed a round of full-spectrum antibiotics.

Cheetah Bob—not my person.

Take It From Me...
- If you feel something is off, trust your intuition.
- When you ask for the truth, be prepared for what you might hear.
- Pay attention to the influences in your partner's life.
- Most strippers are probably cool people who just want to do their job and go home; this one went rogue.
- Learn fancy tongue tricks.

Apache Bob

I graduated from high school two years early. It was a difficult time for me because I never felt like I fit in. By the end of freshman year, I was starting to come into my own, physically. High school is all about cliques and fitting into proverbial boxes: jock, band geek, stoner, popular (aka: mean girls). And although I looked the part of a cheerleader, I was actually a total jock. I was in honors classes but found more inspiration at the beach, which led to countless ditch days with the stoners. Thankfully, school came easily for me and I was able to maintain a 4.0 despite rarely attending class.

I've always felt more comfortable being around people who were older than me, so at school, amongst my peers, I often felt like an outsider looking in. To add fuel to that fire, I was bullied every day by a bunch of psychotic bitches who made it their life's mission to make my life miserable. These girls were legit crazy as fuck, and I was over it. Hi Ladies! Yep, that is my name on the cover of this book! Remember me? Thank you so much for teaching me at such an early age how NEVER to treat people. Oh, and thanks too for inadvertently encouraging me to pursue a career in psychology so I could better understand the inner workings of troubled souls.

Anyway, half-way through my sophomore year, I tested out of school and moved in with my friend Christina and her family. My parents were devastated by my decision, but I desperately wanted to get away and exercise my freedom. Like most teenagers, I found my parents' belief systems to be rigid and stifling to my spirit. I have always been an outside-the-box thinker and this challenged their conservative perceptions. It got to the point where we were constantly hitting heads. I even went as far as researching attorneys to potentially facilitate my emancipation. In the end, it felt too severe to legally separate from my parents who I loved so deeply. The happy medium for me was to live on my own and to preserve our relationships.

As a teenager, I had a vision of becoming a filmmaker so I began taking film classes at a local community college, while working retail at a clothing store in the mall. I saw an ad in the paper to get paid to be a dinner companion. It paid waaaaay more than Wet Seal and, more importantly, I would never have to fold another stupid V-neck again. The job said you had to be eighteen, but I had a fake ID, so I was obviously qualified. I applied and was hired that day.

My first gig as an escort was in Newport Beach, having dinner with a man twenty-five years my senior. I made $150 for an hour of my time, ate two lobster tails, listened to live jazz, and left my first day on the job giggling at how easy it was! Calm your tits, I never slept with any of these desolate businessmen in search of a trophy girl to temporarily soothe their egos. I just had dinner with them and let them pay me. Yawn. Stretch. It felt liberating to be on my own and away from the confines of authority.

By this time, I had been approached about modeling on a few different occasions. But I was skeptical at first, having never really viewed myself as "model material." My sister was always the pretty one and I was more hardcore tomboy. I wasn't used to receiving validation for my looks, until I became an escort. But when my friend, Becky, said her sister knew of an excellent photographer, I figured it couldn't hurt to give the modeling thing a try.

Enter, Apache Bob. I made an appointment to meet with Bob to discuss having my professional pictures taken. This would be only my second time being professionally photographed, and I was nervous.

I drove out to Bob's studio in Huntington Beach, which was actually a warehouse that he had turned into an apartment and art studio. Pulling up to the sketchy-looking entrance, my first thought was that I was probably going to have to tell Bob I wasn't interested in pursuing a career in the porn industry. As it turned out, this wasn't necessary. Bob wasn't into porn after all! He was more of a Native American Demi-God. The dude was tan, with long flowing black locks, and totally ripped in a lean vegan sort of way. I was fascinated by the sheer number of gargoyles that adorned the warehouse and the warlock tapestries he had hanging everywhere. It was actually a beautiful space, not at all like the creepy Dateline episode you're probably imagining.

Bob asked me to go for a walk down Main Street with him to get coffee. We totally hit it off, even though he was twenty-one years older than me. As I write this, I fully realize it sounds completely shady, but it wasn't. Bob and I began spending time together and I moved in with him a few weeks later. This sounds even shadier. Calm down. We would only kiss (except for one time when we dry humped). It was way more of a spiritual connection than it was physical.

Bob was extremely involved in the community and was often celebrated for his charity work. He was a good man, on a mission to make the world a better place. I dug it. Because his art appealed to the more spiritually inclined, his customers were an assortment of interesting characters, including tarot card readers, self-proclaimed witches, and shamans. One of his regulars owned a spiritual center and invited us to a ceremony she was hosting. As we arrived, even from the parking lot, I could feel something inside of me shift. The smell of burning sage and flickering candles had me intrigued. We ascended a narrow staircase and entered a dimly lit room filled with people chanting on yoga mats. It was here that I met my first psychic. She was at least twenty years older than me, but something about her felt timeless.

The next afternoon, the psychic woman came by the studio. She was interested in renting space from Bob. I asked her if she would do a private reading for me, and she sat me down, held my hands, and began immediately. I remember crying the entire time because everything she told me, resonated deeply. I had no words, only tears. It's difficult to explain, but I felt a sense of coming "home." Parts of me that always felt so different from other people, including my family, were finally making some sense. I took deep comfort in knowing that there were other people out there like me.

She told me that in a past life, I was a "Socrates" type, who intuitively knew things, and desperately wanted to teach them. Apparently, my throat had been shackled by authorities in order to silence me. (You don't have to feel sorry for me. I am definitely making up for lost time during my medieval lifetime. I straight up get paid to talk and channel pearls of wisdom in this incarnation. It's SO killer.) Before she left that day, she also told me that I was an empath and that I needed to take extra care of myself because of it.

This information reverberated throughout my entire being. Everything about this new world and way of seeing life felt so right to me. I began to understand why I had never really felt as though I fit in before. I realized that I had made the decision to leave home and school early so I could finally be free to express myself, my interests, and my queries about life.

On the other hand, I was also totally spooked. This was a major disruption to the programming of my conservative family, and I questioned if I had accidentally stumbled into a cult or some bizarre shit. The thing was…everything finally made sense. This was where I belonged. Not like in a warehouse necessarily, but with people who shared these beliefs.

As Bob and I grew closer, he became a cheerleader for my spirit. He encouraged me to express myself, use my voice, and live life the way I felt was best for me. I met Bob's ten-year-old son and his ex-wife. They were all so loving with each other. It was a true gift to witness that break-ups don't have to be nasty.

At first, when no one knew how old I was or what kind of relationship I had with Bob, things were fine. When the women in Bob's circle began to realize we were romantically involved, I began to sense some major jealousy and judgment. Perhaps it was youth or naivety, but being with Bob never felt strange to me. In fact, I felt a sense of overwhelming peace as I uncovered more of who I was. Bob always treated me with the utmost respect and kindness.

But, as you might imagine, my parents were rip-roaring pissed when they discovered my new living arrangements. They shut that shit down faster than I could blink. I am not sure if it was the gargoyles or just the fact that their seventeen-year-old daughter was shacking up with a thirty-eight-year-old photographer. My parents can be totally dramatic. I tried to explain to them that Bob and I never actually boned, we just kind of rubbed off on each other once. No dice.

Eventually, I lost touch with Bob, but am forever grateful to him because he was so instrumental in shaping, feeding, and helping me embrace my spirituality. I know Apache Bob played an essential role in my becoming a healer. To this day, when I facilitate sacred healing ceremonies, I pay tribute to him. These ceremonies have changed my life and I am honored to host them at my mountain retreat in Colorado.

Apache Bob—A great person, but not *my* person.

Take It From Me...
- Escorting is not an altogether unfortunate business venture.
- Bullies suck!
- Not all warehouses are used for porn. *Most are, though.
- Age doesn't always matter.
- We are spiritual beings having a human experience.

Counterfeit Cop Bob

I met Counterfeit Cop Bob while on Spring Break at my parents' vacation home in Lake Havasu. I was relaxing on my parents' boat when some cute guys started making laps on jet skis to flirt with my friend Becky and me. I lifted my shades to get a better look at one studly piece of man flesh in particular; he was tan, muscular, sexy, and obviously the alpha of the group because all his buddies were following him.

At eighteen, I already knew I had a thing for alphas. I think it's in my DNA. My dad is an alpha, his dad was an alpha, my mom's dad was an alpha. And by the time I was in third grade, I was running my first profit-earning candy company so I think it is safe to assume that I am an alpha too.

As I watched these hotties ride circles around our boat, I thought to myself how lucky I was to find my Prince Charming this way. I mean, some women have to wait until they are in their late sixties to meet their soulmate…after he has convinced her he is Nigerian royalty and she has sent him her entire life savings, only to discover the "Nigerian Prince" is really a pasty pervert in Arkansas hiding behind his keyboard in his mother's basement.

So needless to say, I was positively elated that I met my soulmate when I was young and broke.

Bob lived in the super ritzy Belmont Shores in Long Beach while I was attending a music program at UCLA. Score! That was only a twenty minute drive. Maybe we were really meant to be! We exchanged numbers and wasted no time making a plan to go out once we returned home. I was super excited, but a little overwhelmed when I did the math and realized I would be planning our wedding right around the time I would be graduating with the first of my many degrees. I also made a mental note that I would clearly have to be the breadwinner here since Bob was a police officer. A noble career for sure, but a cop salary wasn't going to cover my weekly seaweed colonics, placenta facials, and team of hybrid housekeeper-nannies.

Bob picked me up from my sister's house for our first date. I was somewhat indecisive about what to wear. I had met him while wearing a bikini and he had no idea what I actually looked like with clothes on. At eighteen, it was easy to meet and hang out without giving any thought to the fact that I was half naked. Now, you couldn't pay me enough money to meet a guy in my bikini. You have to EARN the privilege of seeing my stretch marks. Besides, now that I am about twice that age, I have happily parted ways with my bikinis and gracefully graduated to what I call my one-piece "comfort suit."

Bob and I chatted on the way to the restaurant. He was nice-looking, broad-shouldered (I love, no, I require broad shoulders), and gregarious. A deep feeling of contentment coursed through my uterus. I wondered how he felt about converting to Judaism. Everything was going absolutely swimmingly when Bob randomly asked me how I felt about penis enlargements. I could feel my brain brakes come to a screeching halt. Wait. What?

"Well, I have honestly never given them much thought (like any), but I think that people should do what makes them happy or feel better about themselves." I watched as a visible wave of relief passed over Bob. Shit. Ever the optimist, I assumed Bob was simply exaggerating the predicament. I decided to play it safe and fought the urge to probe (no pun intended).

Bob and I had been dating a couple months when I discovered my soul's true work in this life. Some people are passionate about animal rights, others enjoy deworming orphans in third world countries, and some folks have total hard-ons for preserving fossil fuels, but not me. Nope. My newest plight was fundraising for penis enlargements. I was going to devote my entire life to helping dicks. You're welcome, ladies.

I didn't tell Bob this because I truly adored everything else about him and I didn't want to give him a bigger complex (just a bigger penis). I am classy like that. And even though I had admittedly had light-flow tampons inside me that were bigger than him, we were definitely compatible in other ways. It also helped that I am not really an internal orgasm girl anyway. I figured he could make up for his shortcomings in other ways.

Bob still lived with his parents and older brother. He explained his master plan to me: Save his cop salary over the next two years and make a sizable down payment on a house. I suspected he was also saving for his peen surgery, which I fully supported. I quickly became comfortable with his family and would often go stay with them when I had breaks from school. Bob would wake up early in the morning, put on his cop uniform, kiss me goodbye, and leave for work. I would sleep another few hours, make my way to the kitchen for coffee, and chat with his mom. In my mind, we were laying the foundation for a nice, simple, wholesome life together, once he got his new penis.

One weekend Bob was taking on an extra shift at the jail, when his best friend, Matt, who was also a police officer, stopped by. I had heard so much about Matt and was thrilled to meet him in person. We hung out for an hour or so and even though Bob had not even proposed to me, I wondered which of my brides-maids I would have Matt escort down the aisle at the wedding. My best friend at the time, Becky, had already claimed Bob's super-hot older brother who had his own fitness show on MTV. I casually remarked how cool it was that both Bob and his BFF were cops. Matt gave me a super weird look.

"What do you mean by 'we are both cops?'"

I stared at Matt like he was stupid and cheerfully said, "That you and Bob are both cops! I think that's really neat!"

Matt gave me a perplexed look, "Stefanie…What are you talking about? Bob isn't a cop. He works at his grandfather's hard-ware store."

I started laughing, "No. He is definitely a police officer. I watch him put on his uniform and badge every morning. He even puts on a big jacket over his uniform before he leaves the house, so he wont draw attention to himself on the way to work!"

"You've got to be kidding me."

"No, seriously. Yesterday, he told me about a drug bust he made, where they arrested a major drug trafficker from Mexico."

Matt paled, "I just told Bob I arrested a major drug trafficker the other night. I have known Bob since we were kids. This doesn't make any sense." A sense of uneasiness washed over me. OMG. No wonder his mom just laughed when I asked her if she worried about her son when he went to work. I am sure him accidentally dropping a can of Grandpa's paint on his fucking foot wasn't keeping her up late at night.

I could tell Matt was unnerved by this, as he began ceaselessly cracking his knuckles. When he got up to leave, he handed me his cell number and told me to call him. He was clearly not happy. I sat there, entirely bewildered and embarrassed. Assuming Matt was telling the truth, I had been played for a complete fool. I gathered my stuff and left before Bob got home.

I called Matt on my drive back to LA. I bombarded him with rapid-fire questions as I desperately tried to uncover if Bob had told me the truth about anything. Matt was very forthcoming with me. I could tell he felt bad for my situation and this was his way of getting revenge on Bob for stealing his hard-earned accomplishments and passing them off as his own. Turns out, Bob had assumed his friend's identity to compensate for his own perceived inadequacies. Not only did I learn that Bob was not a cop, but all of his elaborate stories about graduating top of his class at the police academy were bullshit too. Well duh, you would have to actually attend the police academy.

Later that night, Bob called me and I immediately confronted him. I played it tough, but the truth is, part of me wanted him to have a logical explanation for the mix-up. I didn't want him to be a liar. I was holding out hope for something, anything, to make this okay. But as I listened to him talk in circles, making absolutely no sense, I felt any hope I had slipping away. There was no denying it, Bob was busted.

I am a big believer in giving credit where credit is due. Bob was indeed a masterful liar. I mean he even had a perfectly logical explanation for putting on a big coat over his uniform before leaving the house each morning. This had nothing to do with

25

keeping from being a target, and everything to do with hiding his store-bought cop costume from his family. And I bought the whole story, hook, line, and sinker.

In a stroke of ironic luck, this all happened during the time the band 'The Cranberries' was popular. I used to play their song "Liar" over and over again, belting out the chorus, as if my speakers were somehow to blame. I was living with my cousin at the time. Her poor cat was forced to endure my cathartic shrieking for weeks. I'm sure I probably caused permanent damage to that thing's eardrums. Over the next month or so, every time Bob would try to call, I would simply blast his namesake song, "Liar" into the receiver. He finally got the message and stopped calling.

The irony of this story is I actually liked Bob. The problem was, he didn't like himself. I wouldn't have cared that he worked at a hardware store. Especially, if he planned on inheriting the company and expanding it, like he did with his penis. I come from a long line of entrepreneurs and I could have taught him to franchise and bring home the Benjamins. Thank God that even at my young age, I knew better than to tolerate being lied to. Well, unless of course, I ask someone if I look bloated. I guess Bob compensated for not having a big dick, by acting like one instead.

Counterfeit Cop Bob—not my person.

Take It From Me...
- Size does matter.
- Truth matters more.
- Thank you 90's grunge bands for angsty music.

Fake Navy Seal Bob(s)

The first Fake Navy SEAL Bob I dated was when was I was twenty and living in Colorado. My roommate's boyfriend had a super cute, older brother and the four of us were always hanging out. Bob told me he was a former Navy SEAL, but didn't like to talk about his war stories. I assumed he probably had some major PTSD and deeply respected his choice not to discuss his past. In fact, I was so respectful of his service to our country that I never even brought it up with my roommate or her boyfriend.

I am all about self-love, but Bob took this to a whoooole new level even by my standards. I distinctly remember him sitting at my vanity one day while staring at himself in the mirror. Looking deep into his own eyes Bob whimsically said, "I love you, Stefanie." I made a weird face and quickly changed the subject. I knew I didn't stand a chance since he was so madly in love with himself.

One evening, on our way to see a movie, we got into an argument while waiting at a red light. Bob decided this would be an ideal time to call his buddy, right in the middle of our conversation. Pissed, I grabbed the phone from him and put it on speaker and said, "Bob is going to have to call you back." Except there was no one there. WTF. "Um Bob, you aren't talking to anyone…"

Bob snatched the phone out of my hand and pretended to call his "friend" back. Hi. If you are going to do something as stupid as fake call a friend to avoid a fight with your girlfriend, at least think it through a little bit. Dum-Dum didn't even take the most obvious line of defense and pretend to be disconnected. If this exemplified the amount of mental fortitude and problem solving required to be a NAVY SEAL, our country was in big trouble.

We pulled up to the next intersection, and when I asked Bob to put his call on speaker phone to actually prove he was really talking to someone this time, he suddenly jumped out of my car and took off running. Like full on sprinting away from me. I watched with utter fascination and curiosity as he then proceeded to scale a tall brick wall. Well goddamn, I thought, maybe the dude actually was a Navy SEAL. I totally couldn't do that.

I drove around for a few minutes trying to find Bob before I got bored and split. When I got home, I told my roommate and her boyfriend what happened. They both looked at me in disbelief and asked me what I was talking about. Apparently, Bob was not a SEAL, nor had he ever even been in the military.

Bob eventually surfaced and repeatedly tried to call me. While I never spoke with him again, I had no idea that this experience would serve as foreshadowing for another incident years down the road…

I was thirty-six and living in Atlanta when I met some guy online who invited me to an Aerosmith concert. This Bob assured me he had great seats, so I agreed to go. Aerosmith is one of my Mom's all-time favorite bands; she would have killed me if I didn't go. To his credit, he wasn't lying about the seats. We were literally so close to the stage that I could see the sweat on Steven Tyler's brow.

Bob and I had a great time and he proved to be an amazing kisser. We went out a few more times and he informed me he was a former Navy SEAL. He told me all sorts of elaborate details about his training. I didn't necessarily *not* believe him, but I also was not falling for this bullshit again. I decided to have a background check done on him to ensure I wasn't inadvertently dating another psych case.

Even though his background results were still pending, I said yes when Bob invited me out on another date. We decided to meet over at his house before we went out to dinner. I got all dressed up and drove over to his place.

I was a little surprised by all the SEAL paraphernalia adorning his walls; the dude definitely had a decorative theme going on. There were little military figurines everywhere and Navy SEAL books all over. I casually plucked a book off his shelf and watched as he became instantly agitated. I worried that he was suffering from PTSD since his mood instantly changed. Bob went and got a beer and plopped down in his recliner. I reminded him about dinner, but he just kept going out to his garage to grab more beer. After an hour of watching him drink beers and no indication we would be leaving for our dinner date, I finally decided I'd had enough, and left. This was definitely not going to be my life—and not just because I loathe figurines.

I had already completely forgotten about Bob, when a week later the results came in…he was never in the military. So basically, I managed to date two, repeat TWO, ego maniacs who were so desperate for attention and adoration that they actually manufactured fake personas to compensate for their insecurities and shortcomings.

Fake Navy SEAL Bobs—not my people.

I am a patriot and have a profound love for this country. My Dad was in Viet Nam, and I have heard the stories. I am deeply humbled and grateful for the service true military men and women contribute. It really pisses me off that there are impostors out there collecting praise from unsuspecting people. If you ever find yourself dating a SEAL, keep in mind that only about 5% of recruits actually make the cut. If something smells fishy, you may have a slimy salamander on your hands versus an actual SEAL.

Take It From Me...
- Background checks are a good idea.
- Get to know friends and family of anyone you are considering as a potential partner.
- Date people with integrity and a strong sense of self-worth.
- Sweaty Steven Tyler is totally awesome.
- The men and women who serve our country deserve profound appreciation—and not insecure impersonators.

Fiancé Bob

I met Fiancé Bob when I was working on my undergrad in Colorado. I had just turned twenty-one and was out at a bar with my girlfriend, Alicia, when I spotted this tall drink of water. He was wearing a red baseball hat and was schooling everyone at the pool table. I watched girl after girl try to talk to him and earn his attention. He didn't seem even the slightest bit interested. I wondered if he might be gay, but he had a sexy, very hetero swagger to him. Alicia saw my interest and dared me to go talk to him. Anyone who knows me, knows I cannot resist a dare. I narrowed my eyes and shrugged as I made my way over to him.

For the life of me, I cannot remember what I said to start the conversation, but kudos to me because he didn't shoo me away like he had with the parade of girls that came before me. Bob and I ended up talking and flirting. It didn't take long to figure out Bob was the "cool guy on campus." He was pre-med at the local private university with plans to attend medical school. By the end of the night, we had exchanged numbers.

On our first date, we went to the same college pub where we had met just a few nights prior. Bob and I talked so much that we never even ordered dinner. We sat in our booth, love-smacked, until they turned the lights on and kicked us out. Then we walked back to his apartment where we said goodbye at his doorstep. Bob gave me a hug and closed the door. I quickly turned on my heels and ran back. I knocked on his door, and we had our first kiss. Great kisser and pre-med. I was on cloud 9,000!

The next time we went out, we went to a party together. At the end of the night, Bob came over to my house and spent the night. Stop. I know what you are thinking, but we really did sleep. Okay, so we made out a little (or a lot) but we really did sleep. We eventually did make love, but it wasn't that night. The next morning, I texted my sister, who lived across the street, to let her know that I had a hottie over. She came running over to peek under the blanket—like Bob was a newborn baby—and tell me how cute he was.

After this, Bob and I were inseparable. We would meet at the library to study, host Taco Tuesdays with our friends, and leave parties early to go sit in the car and listen to song lyrics. Bob would often leave me sweet love notes or bring me a flower and breakfast in bed after his early morning class. One time, Bob left a single rose and a note on my windshield. The note had an address with driving directions. I hopped in the car, having no idea where I was headed, only to arrive twenty-five minutes later at one of Denver's finest hotels downtown. Bob surprised me with a romantic overnight getaway and had thoughtfully packed all my stuff, including my water pic, two toothbrushes, floss, and mouthwash so I could spend my full twenty minutes maintaining my oral routine.

Our relationship was like a storybook romance. I learned that Bob had never had a girlfriend before and was saving himself for the woman he would marry. Sure, he had hooked up with girls, but he had never had a real relationship because he told himself as a young boy that the first girl he made his girlfriend would be the same woman he would marry.

Bob and I literally checked off every box for being the "perfect couple." We were both young, attractive, and ambitious. He was going to be a plastic surgeon and I was going to be a shrink. Our families and friends were thrilled, and I was happy too. It was pretty obvious that I had found the ideal guy to settle down with. We were crazy about each other and everyone loved us together.

Months went on, and as the novelty of the relationship wore off, a small gnawing feeling would occasionally eat at me. I longed to connect with Bob on a deeper, more soulful level. I desperately longed to grow and be challenged, but instead I felt stagnant. I also had no idea how to communicate my need, since I didn't fully understand what I was feeling. At twenty-one, I did not have the emotional vocabulary to identify, much less articulate what was going on inside of me. So, all that came out was misguided frustration.

I have always been the kind of person who derived deep pleasure from enlightening, thought-provoking conversations. In fact, even at sixteen, my friend Becky and I would sit in my car and talk for hours instead of going to high school parties or football games. This sort of connection with others, exploring life's meaning, our purpose for being here, and our philosophies about being human is what sustains me. It's like candy for my spirit. Without it, I feel starved, and anyone who knows me will attest to the fact that when I am hungry, it ain't pretty.

I am not sure why this sort of connection comes more easily with some people than others. I desperately wanted to be able to get to this place with Fiancé Bob. I felt ashamed when I found myself attracted to other men who could possibly fill this need.

Bob was very intellectual, top of his class actually, but we just couldn't connect on the psychological level I craved.

As I was struggling, I remember nervously confiding in a couple of girlfriends that I wasn't sure I belonged with Bob. My friends told me I was crazy and that I had the relationship of their dreams. I felt confused and guilty for having these doubts, especially when I was with such a good man who adored me.

Desperate for clarity, I sought advice from one of my professors who had become a friend. She told me that no one was ever going to be able to provide me with everything and that I could find that kind of stimulation in my work and with colleagues. I remember being disappointed that this wasn't an inherent part of love, but I saw her point; needs could be filled in different ways. I was just going to start having soulful conversations with my vibrator after we got it on.

The last person I ever confided in about this was a girl who was a close mutual friend to me and Bob. I will never forget how she begged me to stay in the relationship because she was so certain that what I had was the perfect relationship, one that movies are made of. She had recently lost her fiancé in a car accident and desperately wanted us to stay together so we could have the love that she felt had been stolen from her.

I felt so guilty. What was wrong with me? Why couldn't I just be happy? Bob was the ultimate catch. In this moment, I chose to ignore my intuition and brushed my feelings aside. Because I did not yet understand the strength of spirit, I actually believed that my spirit would quietly retreat and stay put. Instead, my spirit began knocking louder and I didn't know how to silence her.

One night, Bob and I got into an argument and I refused to let him into my house. He was so intent on talking to me that he climbed up on the balcony and proceeded to pound on my bedroom door. I called the police, hoping they would make him get down and leave. Well, Colorado law is no joke in matters like this. Despite my begging them to let him go, they ended up arresting Bob, and he had to spend the night in jail. I bailed him out the next morning. It was awful and never my intention. Bob's family paid a fortune to have it sealed and we found ourselves back together. We were so young and immature, and at the same time, it seemed like we were doing everything we were "supposed to do."

I felt like something was seriously wrong with me for feeling unfulfilled when I had a partner that women dream of. I continued to convince myself that I would be stupid to leave him. Around the same time, I started to become sick. It seemed like I was at the doctor's office every other day. I was constantly fatigued and my body just ached. There were days when I could not get out of bed. I had recurring respiratory infections and major intestinal issues. I saw countless doctors. At one point, I was on fourteen different medications at the same time. Nothing was working and nobody could figure out what was wrong with me. I was flying back and forth to California to see various specialists.

Bob took care of me the entire time and never once complained. His commitment to me was unwavering. When Bob's friends flew in from New York to go skiing, he canceled his plans to stay home and take care of me. He was fired from his job because he called in so many times to stay home and help me. Bob was so good to me; he would literally give me enemas at night. Such a strangely unattractive thing for two extremely attractive people to be doing together, but he freaking did it.

One morning, Bob took me to my colonoscopy and endoscopy appointment. I had to starve myself for two days prior and drink a laxative called "Go-Lightly," which is actually grounds for false advertising since the name is a total fucking lie. It was more like "Go-Violently" and honestly, I am not sure my butthole has yet to forgive me for this betrayal. I woke up from the procedure and was positively ravenous. The doctor instructed Bob to only give me soft, bland foods. But, because I am a total brat, I convinced him to get me Cinnabun and chocolate milk.

I started shoveling food into my face and everything was fine for approximately two minutes before I screamed for Bob to pull over. I puked my brains out all over the side of his car and onto the curb. I barfed so much that I would have made a drunk sorority girl envious. And still, he stayed…

After Bob graduated college, we decided to move back to my hometown in California. We wanted to be closer to my parents and the medical specialists I had been seeing. We moved in with my parents while we were having our house built. Bob began working for my family business and the love my parents had for him grew even stronger. Bob felt like family, and to make it official, he secretly asked my father if he could marry me. My dad agreed (duh).

On the day Bob planned to propose, I had just walked in the door after a long day at work. Bob was uncharacteristically rushing me to get ready. I was super annoyed because I didn't understand why he was being so pushy. We ended up getting into a huge fight and out of sheer frustration, Bob threw the ring and the box at me. I was totally stunned and positively pissed that he couldn't contain his frustration. Having an engagement ring thrown at me was never in the realm of possibility for the way a man would one day propose to me.

After some tears were shed, we regrouped. Bob explained that we had to rush because he had planned a sunset cruise for us, and we had to make it to the harbor before the boat set sail. I got my ass in gear, did my makeup in the car, and we made it to the boat with only three minutes to spare. Two glasses of champagne coupled with the outrageously gorgeous sunset view from the yacht, and our nerves were happily put at ease. We enjoyed a lobster dinner, chocolate cake, and a slow dance on the deck. It was then that Bob got down on one knee and asked me to marry him. I said yes.

When we told everyone the exciting news, they told us it was a "fairytale romance." A week before moving into our new house, we sat on the floor of our soon-to-be master bedroom and lit a candle. Over candlelight, we shared our dreams for the future and what we would create in our new home. We walked into each of the empty rooms that we planned to fill with children. Our children. This is still one of my favorite memories with Bob.

Even though Bob treated me like gold, my longing for something deeper and more soulful persisted. I felt myself becoming increasingly agitated. Despite being physically attracted to Bob, I didn't want to have sex anymore. This is when I learned my vagina is directly linked to my psyche. If my spirit is not turned on, nothing else is. Bob and I were in couple's therapy at twenty-two. I didn't know why I couldn't be happy. I was living the dream that had been ingrained in me since I was a child.

Everything came crashing down on Valentine's Day. I walked into our house and immediately thought it was on fire. It turned out that Bob had rented a fog machine and was trying to set the stage for a romantic evening. Instead of being amused by his botched attempt at romance, I became completely unhinged. I was so irritated and entirely ungrateful for his gesture. I ended up breaking up with him and calling off the wedding right there, in our foggy kitchen.

Bob was absolutely gutted. Everyone was stunned. I knew I had broken the rules and I felt terrible. I had underestimated the strength of my spirit. I had sought counsel from everyone except her.

Bob moved out and rented a house. We hung out a bit here and there, but never got back together. I ran into him when I went to a movie with my Aunt Jan and he was with another girl. I pretended that it didn't hurt, said hi, and watched as my aunt gave him a huge hug. Everyone loved Bob. I was crushed, but I remained resolute that I had made the right decision.

A few months later, I began receiving phone calls in the middle of the night from some girl named Melissa. It was obvious this chick was totally wasted. She would slur as she screamed horrible things at me and then hang up. I eventually learned she was Bob's new girlfriend. One evening she drunk-called to inform me that they had gotten into an argument and Bob told her he would never love her the way he had loved me. I felt the burn of regret, but again, deep down, I had to trust that I had made the right decision.

One evening I went out to a bar in Newport Beach with some girlfriends. I walked outside to have a cigarette. Yes, I used to smoke. And yes, it's gross. And triple yes, I am beyond grateful that I quit over a decade ago. Anyway, there were two guys and a girl standing on the patio, and I asked them for a light. The girl and I began talking and she told me her name was "Kristen" and that she was a hairdresser. I finished my cigarette and went back inside.

Later that night, I received another call while I was getting ready for bed. The woman said, "You are such a dumb bitch. You are so fucking stupid." It turns out that the girl I was talking to on the bar patio was Melissa. She had recognized me from a photo Bob had and because I had no idea what the lunatic drunk calling me actually looked like, she pretended to be someone else to my face. Sister was literally psychotic. I called Bob to tell him to make her leave me alone.

Eventually the woman stopped calling and I learned just how dysfunctional their relationship had been. I tried repeatedly to talk to Bob over the years. I desperately wanted to explain to him how sorry I was and why it didn't work out with us, but Bob wanted no part of me. I did not leave this relationship unscathed either. I was so worried I would never find anyone who loved me the way Bob did. Every failed relationship from thereon out reinforced this fear. There were times when I became so afraid that I had made the worst decision of my life and that my punishment would be being alone forever.

Years later when I was living in Atlanta, I called Bob. We spent an hour talking. He told me that he had left the corporate world to go road-tripping and soul-searching for a few months. I had hoped it would cultivate a friendship, but we drifted apart again. One of the greatest heartbreaks of my life has been Bob not wanting to have any relationship with me. For me, he was such a meaningful and important part of my life. I wanted us to remain in contact, but he just refused. Maybe it was his way of getting revenge. Or maybe it was too painful for him to be my friend. I guess I will never know, and the truth is that this still hurts to this day. So many words have remained unsaid. And now that I have the emotional vocabulary, spiritual awareness, and ability to speak vulnerably, I want so badly to explain to Bob what actually happened—for his sake and for mine.

The last time I saw Bob, I was living in Atlanta and had flown out to visit a girlfriend in San Diego for New Year's Eve. We were walking back to our hotel when I heard someone yell, "Stefanie!" I knew it was him. Ironically, in a weird twist of fate, I had just shown my girlfriend an old picture of Bob an hour prior, while at dinner. I turned around and saw Bob was with a woman

DR. STEFANIE KLEINE AND ERIN MORONI

who he introduced as his fiancée. I congratulated them and told her she was marrying a gem. The woman had a beautiful accent, and I asked where she was from. She tersely said, "The world." I awkwardly nodded and we said goodbye. I asked my girlfriend if she noticed how aloof his fiancée was to me. My girlfriend started laughing and said, "Well, Stef, he did recognize you from the back. Wouldn't you be?" Fair enough.

After Bob and I broke up, I made a vow to myself that I would use my voice in all future relationships, that I would speak my truth, and that I would bravely express my needs, no matter how clunky my communication might be. I also promised to never settle. If I was willing to walk away from such a wonderful man who truly adored me, I surely was not going to ever settle for anything less than what I knew my heart and spirit needed.

Fiancé Bob – An incredible person, but not my person.

Take It From Me…

- We deserve to be in relationship with people who treat us well.
- Vulnerable communication is critical for a lasting, fulfilling relationship.
- Listen to your spirit more than you listen to outside influences.
- Honor your needs and use your voice to ask for them.
- The connection between mind and body is undeniable. You can often heal your physical ailments by healing your spirit.
- We often think we know who we are and what we want in our 20's. That commonly changes or doesn't authentically reveal itself until we are a little older. Research shows that marriages later in life have greater success.

40

Sugar Daddy Bob

When I met Sugar Daddy Bob, I had recently called off my wedding. I just wanted to have shameless fun and not be seriously involved with anyone. I would like to think how I acted in this relationship was because I was only twenty-four at the time and my brain was still technically growing. Still, ugh…I am not proud.

I met Sugar Daddy Bob online. He was eight years older than me, born in Italy, and was the heir to a major manufacturing dynasty. Additionally, Bob was also a certifiable genius. The dude worked in the field of quantum physics and was an actual rocket scientist, thus proving that not all Italians are in the mafia. I mean most are, but some definitely are not. Yes. I was equally stunned to learn this.

Bob definitely lacked in social skills, and I couldn't discern if it was a cultural barrier or simply because his brain operated on an entirely different level than that of the average human being. I rationalized that his personality was tolerable since he owned a beach cottage in Laguna Beach, a mansion in Pasadena, a bright red convertible Mercedes, and could afford to entertain me. This was exactly the kind of distraction I needed to shush my runaway bride blues. Almost immediately, Bob wanted to spend a ton of time with me. I am pretty sure he had been navigating his life as a party of one and was thrilled to have a new playmate.

I still loved Fiancé Bob and didn't want to sleep with anyone, so I lied and told Sugar Daddy Bob that I was a virgin and was saving myself for marriage. This only strengthened his postulation that I was the ideal mate for him since I was quite the arm candy in my early twenties. Bob surprised me one morning after brunch, by handing me the keys to his Mercedes.

Bob said he wanted me to enjoy it and he was happy driving his Lexus SUV. He also told me that there was a surprise for me in the glove box. Turns out, he put his credit card in the glove box for me, with a monthly allowance. A very generous monthly allowance. The dude wanted to lock this shit down, and even though I had no intention of sticking around long-term, I went along for the ride.

Bob's family was visiting from Italy, so we met for dinner. Despite the hilarious language barrier, we got along fine. I am positive this had more to do with the fact that they were just happy to see their socially awkward son with an actual woman. I totally caught Mama Italy checking out the girth of my hips to see if I was suitable to bear future male heirs to inherit the family fortune. Whatever.

After a couple months, Bob really ratcheted up the ol' anger button. He started to become uber controlling and always wanted to know where I was or where I was going. I am certain that he believed with the right amount of money, he could purchase me and have full say in what I did or did not do. One of the final straws for me was when I told him I was considering a boob job, and he made some comment about me getting liposuction instead. Because he was so socially inept, I don't even think he understood that this was hurtful.

As time went on, I began to notice Bob getting boastful and trying to compete with me over everything. Reminding me that he could calculate the rotation of the earth's gravitational pull and solve fifth grade math word problems in Mandarin Chinese was his way of putting me in my place. Yippee. You win, Bob.

Having no idea that I was quickly losing interest in the relationship, or maybe as a Hail Mary of sorts, Bob took me to Newport Coast one afternoon and told me to pick out a lot for the mansion he was going to have built for us. Although a mansion in Newport Coast is a dream to most people, the thought of spending my life in servitude to him and the nose-picking nerdy kids we would have, made me cringe. I knew I had to crush his soul and I wasn't looking forward to it.

I told my friend Jana that I was going to end it with Bob. Jana demanded that I return the car and his credit card. I fucking KNEW I shouldn't have told her; that girl totally gets in my head.

In a moment of selfishness and partial revenge for all the times that Bob insulted me (knowingly and unknowingly), I went out and bought a bunch of gift cards with my allowance money. I then called Bob and broke it off. As I predicted, Bob was totally heartbroken. I actually felt super guilty and returned the car and his credit card. To this day, my Dad doesn't understand why I didn't just make it work with Sugar Daddy Bob. He doesn't get why I couldn't just teach Bob social skills. After all, I am a trained psychologist.

Oh, Dad, believe me, there are moments when I am so disappointed in love and feel like completely giving up. And in those moments, I figure why not just settle and be with a man who can at least provide a super cushy lifestyle? But the truth is, I would rather be broke than feel captive to a lonely marriage.

Sugar Daddy Bob—not my person.

Take It From Me...
- Lying will make you feel terrible.
- Refuse to be controlled in any relationship.
- Real men do not compete with women.
- It's better to be alone than feel lonely with someone.
- You can't buy love.

Masturbating Bob

I met Masturbating Bob while I was on a girls' trip in Palm Springs. Calm down. He wasn't masturbating when I met him; this would have been a giant red flag that even I couldn't miss. We actually met in a much classier way…at a really nice bar. It totally reminded me of *The Notebook*. (If *The Notebook* took place in a swanky nightclub outside of LA and if, like, I had dementia.)

I chatted up this tasty little Middle Eastern dish of a man for a few minutes before we realized that we only lived about thirty minutes away from one another. Since he was Persian and I am Jewish, our kids would obviously be getting nose jobs for their eighteenth birthdays, and I would definitely have to find a skilled pediatric eyebrow threader for their uni-brows. There was also the issue of significant historical turmoil between our respective peoples since the beginning of time…BUT maybe we were the chosen ones predestined to unite our warring nations!

After returning from my girls' trip, Bob and I reconnected and proceeded to go on a couple dates. It was so nice to go out with a man who shared my appreciation for falafel, hummus, and baklava. I was working on my Master's degree at Pepperdine at the time, so he would drive from his Beverly Hills condo to pick me up in his meticulously clean Audi (which would subsequently serve as the catalyst for my 16-year fetish for German luxury vehicles.)

Bob proved to be rather beguiling with his charm, ambition, impeccable fashion sense, and expensive imported cologne. He was intriguing, and I enjoyed being around him. In fact, I liked him so much that I started Googling stylish burkas in between classes and began to entertain the notion of walking ten paces behind him. (Just kidding! I could never wear one of those things unless I was recovering from a face-lift.)

I decided to invite Bob to be my date at Becky's wedding so I could watch him gaze longingly at me while they recited their vows. I have been to dozens of weddings and I never tire of watching my dates become misty-eyed during the old mandatory reading from Corinthians. Everyone knows traditional societal mores suggest this is the only permissible time for male vulnerability to surface, and I deeply relish in this experience.

Bob and I had a lovely time at the wedding. My friends liked him; he was sociable and fun. I caught moments where I was certain that Bob was envisaging marrying me and merging DNA. I tilted my head in bewilderment because I was slowly falling for him as well. I suspected his heritage had influenced his chosen career path of brokering mergers and acquisitions, and I was considering becoming his property.

I invited him back to my place after the reception to watch a movie. We sat on my bed, turned on the TV, and started making out a little bit. I sweetly informed Bob that although he was an amazing kisser and I was really fond of him, I was not ready to have sex with him. ANNNND this is when the scale tipped to totally bizarre. Bob began fidgeting with his belt, and then twisting and turning to get his pants off, while still lying next to me on my bed. Once he had undressed himself, he began masturbating. In my bed. Right next to me.

Laughing nervously, I asked, "Ummm...What are you doing!?" Bob kept stroking himself and said calmly in a condescending tone, "Stefanie, if we can't masturbate in front of each other, we will never be able to have a relationship. There are more important things to work through in a relationship." What the hell did that even mean? My entire body stiffened with awkward uneasiness. Not knowing what to do, I rolled over and pretended to sleep like one of those weird fainting goats.

Was this really fucking happening? I was planning on staying home and raising his hairy children. Of course, I was still going to buff my muff, but I was just going to do it like every other mom does, right before they pick up the kids from the school carpool line. No one does this in front of their partner. The whole point of masturbation is NOT to get performance anxiety.

Finally, Ol' Rosy Palms managed to charm his cobra. He moaned and immediately started snoring. I was so confused. Did I not receive the memo about this progressive sexual movement? Was this a peculiar litmus test of sorts? And even more unsettling... what in the hell did he do with his batter? He literally just jerked off on my 700-thread count, European sheets.

Masturbating Bob called me the next day to set up another date. I told him I was busy...for the rest of my life.

Masturbating Bob—not my person.

*Author's Note:
Looking back on my experience with this man, I am able to see it for what it truly was. I was put in a position where I felt dishonored,

scared, and uncomfortable. I had trusted him because he was older and "more sophisticated" in my eyes.

Part of me wanted to please this man. Even though I was not ready for sex, I wanted to show him I was sexy and could one day, pleasure him. I wondered if I should kiss him or touch him to ensure he was still turned on. This is what society had taught me to do. And another part of me, knew the whole thing felt wrong.

This man did not care about how he made me feel in that moment. He was preoccupied with meeting his own needs. He took advantage of my genuine nature, my innocence, and the situation. His lack of insight and empathy was enough for me to realize I could never be with him.

For me, sex is intended to be beautiful, meaningful, and even sacred. It is a precious gift that accompanies human existence and having a body. Most importantly though, it is a reciprocal exchange of vulnerability and trust between human beings. The act of combining bodies in such an intimate way is so powerful that our souls will quickly alert us when boundaries are crossed. We owe to it to ourselves to listen to these internal alarms.

I was admittedly confused for many years after this incident. Should I have handled the situation better? Should I have done something differently? Was it my fault? Had I misled him? The answer is emphatically NO. A victim's reaction to sexually inappropriate behavior does not necessitate a defense or an explanation. If something feels wrong to you, then it is wrong. I was supposedly such a "strong, confident girl," according to everyone who knew me, so why had I frozen in that moment instead of standing up for myself? Was I that desperate for male approval that I would allow someone to make me feel this bizarrely uncomfortable in my own home?

My guilt has since been replaced with profound gratitude for my inner guidance that told me to feign sleep on that particular day. Who knows how this man would have reacted if he felt judged or admonished by me? Perhaps he may have become hostile or even aggressive? In that moment, my inner being chose to diffuse and de-escalate the situation. And I choose to trust that this was the safest choice.

Take It From Me...

- You cannot fall asleep to the sound of meat slapping unless you are in prison.
- You actually *can* have a relationship with someone without masturbating in front of them.
- Honor what feels right for you.
- Intuition is our greatest compass.
- There is no right or wrong way to respond to sexually inappropriate behavior.

Hurricane Bob

Hurricane Bob and I met online when I was in my mid-twenties. Bob was thirty and a big, strapping guy who had played college football at LSU. He was a fun, larger than life kind of guy, very successful, and generous. We had gone out a few times before he invited me to go to New Orleans with him for Halloween.

Since I didn't really know Bob, I agreed to go with the condition that I could bring my friend Madeline and her boyfriend, Alex, with us. Bob excitedly agreed and even paid for all four of us to fly to Louisiana. I cringed at the idea because I was terrified of flying, but somehow managed to suck it up. I was so excited to explore this new city with my friend and spend time with Bob.

Upon arriving in New Orleans, the very first thing we did was hit up a drive-through liquor store. Not. Even. Kidding. This is a real thing. Apparently, Halloween is a major holiday in New Orleans and it was going to be crazy. (I just had no idea how literally true this would be.) We checked in to the hotel and had dinner.

The next day we decided to go on a ghost tour, since New Orleans is a city of voodoo and spirits. Honestly, I was kind of disappointed. The tour was kind of a rip-off. I only saw one ghost, and it wasn't even a spooky murdered one. It just looked like it died of boring influenza. Whatever.

The next day was Halloween, so I put on the mandatory sexy cat costume that all women wear and we headed over to the French Quarter. Everyone was dressed up in amazing costumes, and beads and boobs were flying everywhere. The enigmatic energy of the city was absolutely insane. I learned that the signature drink in New Orleans was called a "Hurricane." We walked down Bourbon street, going from bar to bar, drinking our "hurricanes" and having an absolute blast.

After hours of partying, we headed back to the hotel. We were staying in adjoining rooms and I went into the bathroom to change out of my costume. I heard the door opening and turned to see Bob barging in. He immediately pinned me up against the wall with his massive body. Bob roughly pulled at my clothes, his penis pressed hard against me, and his breath reeking of alcohol. Terror coursed through my veins as I squealed and tried to wrestle away from him. Madeline heard the commotion and knocked on the door. She then opened it and asked if everything was okay. Bob gruffly told her to get out.

I took advantage of this brief distraction and slid out from under him, ducking out of the bathroom and back into the hotel room. Bob followed me out and immediately pinned me against the wall again, kissing me and trying to take off my clothes right in front of Madeline and Alex. I pleaded with him to stop and looked at my friends to help me. Neither of them moved. I eventually got away from Bob and told him that I wasn't staying here. I packed my stuff and looked at Madeline expectantly, assuming she would follow. She diverted her eyes and I slammed the door in utter disbelief.

I quickly got in a taxi and called to book a flight home since this was before smart phones. I reached into my purse to pull out my credit card and realized I had left it and my ID in the hotel room. Bob had carried them for me while we were out because I didn't want to carry a purse and obviously, my sexy cat costume had no pockets. My heart sank as we turned around to return to the hotel.

I went straight to the front desk and asked for them to send someone up to the room since I was absolutely terrified of Bob. A young bellhop went up there and came back empty handed. Bob refused to give it to him. The shock of what had transpired began to wear off and was quickly replaced with fury. I demanded the front desk call security.

After explaining it to hotel security, hotel policy required a police report be made. Now having to explain this real-life Halloween horror story for the third time, the police listened, took a report, and went up to the room to retrieve my credit card and license. This time Bob gave it to them. Madeline never even came down to check on me. I climbed into another taxi all alone in what was then the "Murder Capital of the United States" and flew home to California at 4:00am, still wearing my sexy cat costume.

While I never spoke to Bob again, I did send a couple of scathing messages to Madeline. I couldn't believe that she and Alex had done absolutely nothing to try and stop that monster. I felt traumatized all over again when I discovered that they had sided with Bob. Via text, Madeline told me I had overreacted to the situation, and that I must have misled Bob in some way. The lack of support from someone I considered to be one of my closest friends was equally, but differently devastating to me than the assault itself. To this day, the smell of alcohol on a man in bed makes me want to vomit.

I realize now that Madeline and Alex were intimidated by Bob. He was older. He was wealthy. He had paid for them to go on the trip. They felt indebted to him. Unfortunately, it ultimately came at the cost of our friendship.

Hurricane Bob—not my person.

Take It From Me…
- You NEVER owe a man sex.
- Real men would NEVER treat a woman this way.
- Stand up for people.
- Surround yourself with fearless women who will always support you.
- Listen to your instincts. If your intuition tells you to fight like holy hell—fight like holy hell.
- Always keep your ID on you.

Foul Ball Bob

My relationship with Foul Ball Bob was the first serious relationship I had with a man I met online. I was living in California and he lived in Pennsylvania. We talked for about a month before we began taking trips across the country to visit each other. At one point, I even went out and stayed with him for about six weeks. Bob treated me like gold and it didn't hurt that he was a great kisser and super fun to look at. Like, seriously, the boy was in shape.

Since things were going so well between us, we decided that Bob should just move out to California so we could be together. Bob put in for a transfer with his job and within weeks, he was living with me in my townhouse. We seamlessly fell into a rhythmic routine of domestic bliss. Holy. Shit. Maybe this online dating thing actually could work! I was seriously stunned that the almighty internet had managed to deliver my long-awaited soulmate right to my front door.

One evening Bob had made an amazing dinner of rockfish stuffed with Maryland crab. We began drinking wine and before I knew it, we were all over each other. Bob lifted up my skirt and we ended up having sex in the kitchen with me bent over the counter. It. Was. Incredible. Like white knuckled, screaming for God, "please don't ever stop" good. We were both entirely in the moment and going at it hard.

Suddenly I felt something hit my thigh and heard a sickening popping noise, which was then immediately followed by a blood curdling scream. I whipped around to see Bob curled up on the floor in absolute agony. I looked at his penis which was quickly beginning to resemble an eggplant. I gasped and covered my mouth. The thing was turning dark purple and swelling.

I stood frozen in disbelief for a moment. I never work out because I don't like to sweat or waste my life, but my legs are fucking SOLID for reasons I cannot explain nor do I understand. Essentially, Bob rammed his dick into a brick wall. Bob's audible moan snapped me back to attention.

In a moment of drunken clarity, I ran for the phone and quickly dialed 911.

"UM HI! OH MY GOD! I BROKE MY BOYFRIEND'S PENIS! CAN YOU PLEASE SEND SOMEONE QUICKLY?"

"Ma'am, can you please repeat that?"

WTF. The 911 operator acted like she had never heard of such a thing. "MY BOYFRIEND BROKE HIS DICK ON MY THIGH! IT IS GETTING REALLY BIG! PLEASE HURRY!"

"Ma'am, can you please put your boyfriend on the phone?"

"NO! HE CAN'T TALK RIGHT NOW! HE IS IN SO MUCH PAIN! OH MY GOD! IT IS SO BIG!!!! PLEASE HELP. IT KEEPS GETTING BIGGER AND I DON'T KNOW WHAT TO DO!"

Bob just lay there groaning while I kept trying to convince her that this wasn't a prank call. About five minutes later, we heard a bunch of sirens come tearing through my quiet little neighborhood.

I ran out to the garage and was immediately greeted by a bunch of super hot firefighters.

They all filtered in and I pointed them towards the kitchen where Bob was still laying on the floor, writhing in pain, without any pants on. I watched the firefighters as they surveyed the scene. Based on the looks of sheer mortification and subtle eye contact with one another, I knew even these hardened first responders had never seen anything like this before.

They asked how this had happened and tried hard not to laugh when I told them. They then took turns feeling how strong my leg was in amazement. Eventually, they got to work taking Bob's vitals.

Two giant guys hoisted Bob up onto a gurney and covered him with a white blanket. (Calm down. They just covered up his dick, not like a dead body. Bob was totally still alive, even though he probably felt like dying.) Anyway, they wheeled him outside and into the ambulance, right by a giant crowd of my nosy-ass neighbors who had congregated on their lawns, trying to surmise what had happened.

I climbed into the ambulance with Bob and kept saying, "I am so sorry! Please don't hate me! I love you! I will figure out how to get more leg fat!" Bob just groaned. OMG. Bob and I had talked about getting married and having babies. What if we couldn't have kids? Shit. This was *not* good.

We arrived at the emergency room where the doctor administered some heavy pain killers and immediately went to work draining Bob's penis. Now unbeknownst to me, if you break your boyfriend's penis, you definitely want to have a urologist called in immediately. We had no idea and when we finally did see a urologist a few days later, the damage had already been done. A little known fact about the male anatomy is that blunt trauma to a penis while it is erect can cause a rupture of the tunica albuginea. If this is not treated, complications include permanent curvature of the penis, fistula, erectile dysfunction, and other issues.

For a long time afterward, Bob could not get hard. Eventually, things began to return to normal, but he was never able to maintain a full erection because of the scar tissue. Over time and some intensive therapy, Bob and I did find some humor in the situation. We were definitely total hits at parties because it was such a great precautionary tale. Eventually however, our romantic relationship began to fizzle out and we began to see each other more as friends. Bob and I split, but I assure you it was not because of his dick. Also, I feel compelled to tell you that my legs are still really muscular regardless of how much I don't exercise. Now if only I could get my tummy in order.

Foul Ball Bob—such a good person, but not my person.

Take It From Me…
- Aim is important, and not just for keeping your butt safe.
- Thigh fat is actually a good thing.
- Always demand to see a specialist when someone's penis gets broken.
- Drunk sex can definitely be hazardous.

Movie Star Bob

I met Movie Star Bob when I was twenty-six and living in Newport Beach. A close girlfriend of mine had met a super nice Italian guy by the name of Nick. Apparently, Nick had grown up with a guy who was now a famous actor and they had remained close friends. Nick encouraged me to meet his actor friend, claiming we would totally hit it off.

I was a little reticent because this man was incredibly well known and I didn't necessarily want to garner any attention, but agreed on account of their persistence. Movie Star Bob and I began exchanging texts and eventually made plans to go out to dinner. Even though it was a little awkward to have everyone staring at us while we ate, I was pleasantly surprised by how intelligent his conversation was.

We left the restaurant and went back to my condo complex where we decided to jump the fence and sneak in after-hours to go sit in the jacuzzi. We stripped down to our undies and climbed in. I quickly learned that Bob was absolutely fixated on conspiracy theories. He launched into story after story ranging from espionage, poisoned water, to politics. Bob would say things like, "You're smart so you probably already know all about chem trails." (I still have no idea what a fucking chem trail even is.) But, to his credit, the man did have a multitude of facts and seemingly authentic sources to support his claims.

Without warning, Bob suddenly switched from conspiracy theories to informing me he could sing opera. I slowly nodded. Okay, well this was a new one. Without warning, the dude began bellowing out the old baritone. I immediately started laughing, much as I always do when my dates randomly begin singing opera. Apparently, we were being too loud because a neighbor yelled at us to, "Shut the fuck up." Bob remained undeterred by the critics in the audience and carried on with his Italiano concerto.

About ten minutes later, the cops showed up. Bob remained completely unfazed by their presence. The police immediately recognized Bob and totally kissed his ass. They told us to stay and enjoy ourselves, but just "keep it down a little bit." Um what?

After a five-minute interlude, Bob resumed his concert. This time, I convinced him that we needed to go back to my house since I didn't want to have piles of dog crap flung at my door the next day. I went into my closet and changed into some comfy clothes. I then rummaged through a stack of clothes that I had accumulated from paramours of the past. Bob was a big guy and I finally found something that I thought might fit him. I walked out, handed him some dry clothes, and went into the bathroom to wash my face and brush my teeth.

I finished my nighttime routine and glanced around my bedroom. The closet door was still shut, and Bob was inside. How long did it take for him to change his clothes? I knocked on the door to make sure he was okay. No answer. I knocked a little louder. Nothing. What the fuck?

My brain began to race. Oh My God. What if a famous movie star just had a heart attack and died in my closet? Or what if the sweat pants I gave him were too tight and he had fallen and hit his head as he was jumping up and down, trying to squeeze into them? Shit. Shit. Shit. I was definitely going to jail. Or even more disturbing—what if he was in there trying on my lingerie? Everybody knows actors can be super eccentric, and the dude had just spent hours vacillating between opera and chem trails. Seriously, anything was possible.

I finally opened the door and peaked in only to discover Bob on my floor in his own underwear, hunched over my upturned laundry basket, snorting lines of cocaine. I closed my eyes and took a deep cleansing breath. I felt relieved that I caught him snorting blow in my closet rather than wearing my g-string. Suddenly the frantic conspiracy theories were beginning to make sense. Dude was a total drug addict. He was so high, he was bordering psychosis. Awesome. How was I going to get this guy out of here?

I obviously didn't want Bob to drive, so I surveyed my room and zeroed in on my bed. The very same bed that Masturbating Bob had been in. I decided that after I got through this night, I was going to drag that fucking mattress outside and light it on fire. Clearly it was possessed and needed to go. I sighed and told Movie Star Bob that I was really tired and pointed to the bed. He made a few sordid attempts to make out with me, but to no avail. Eventually he rolled over and fell asleep.

When I woke up the next morning, Bob was gone. A week or so went by and Bob randomly text me. I politely blew him off and assumed he would eventually get the hint. A few days later, I was in my home office studying late at night when I suddenly heard the all too familiar sound of Italian-opera-high-on-cocaine singing at the top of his lungs.

I quickly ran outside to shut his ass up. The neighbors all had their faces pressed up against their windows trying to observe the spectacle unfolding before them. Bob pleaded with me to come have a drink with him. I definitely did not want to let him inside my house, so I told him I would follow him and have one drink, but that I had to study. This seemed to pacify him as he climbed into his sports car.

I followed Bob to a bar where he proceeded to order us drinks, talk about himself for half an hour, and then spend about twenty minutes in the bathroom doing drumroll...more coke! Eventually I got tired of waiting. I got up and left, never to hear from him again. The next time I saw Bob was years later when he was starring on *Celebrity Rehab With Dr. Drew*. Apparently, he was now accepting less demanding roles.

Movie Star Bob—not my person.

Take It From Me...
- Just say no to drugs. Seriously.
- Do not ever compromise your integrity.
- Entitlement is extremely unattractive.
- Be wary of people who never ask anything about you.
- Conspiracy theories are kind of interesting.
- Italian opera is lovely, but not necessarily a first choice for foreplay.

Child Molester Bob

Now, unlike many of the chapters in this book, this one actually has a happy ending. Not that kind. Gross. It's just that I am still friends with Child Molester Bob to this day. I know what you're thinking, but relax and listen.

Bob and I met at a mutual friend's birthday party ten years ago when I was living in Honolulu. I was there for about eight months, in between doctoral programs. Bob and I discovered we worked near each other, had similar schedules, and had quite a bit in common. Anyway, we totally hit it off. As friends.

Bob was a divorced, single dad, with a six-year-old son. When we met, we were immediately taken with one other. I love when I have these instant connections. Unfortunately, I wasn't particularly physically attracted to Bob, so our feelings were not completely in alignment. I firmly placed him in the "buddy" category.

Bob and I would spend our days off walking along the beach, listening to music on my oceanfront patio, and exploring the magic of the island. Bob was a true friend, the kind who helps you move and even comes over to help you build an IKEA nightmare of a dresser. Why do those bastards look so easy to assemble? I swear

I get home, open the packaging, and feel like a complete moron who would have better luck solving a Rubik's cube with one hand... without saying "fuck" once.

Bob was one of the sweetest men I had ever met, and he never turned out to be a stalker or chronic masturbator. He was just a genuinely good human. Slowly, but surely, he grew on me. Eventually, I caved and decided to give romance a shot. I am an Aquarius, so I naturally embrace change, in fact, I crave it. I figured it might actually be nice to date someone who wasn't a total self-absorbed prick for a change.

Bob and I had gone on a few dates when we made plans to see a movie one weekend. The babysitter canceled last minute, so we decided to just take his son with us. Bob looked incredibly relieved by my flexibility (mental, not physical you dirty birdies), and I could tell this only amplified his desire for me to be the glue that fixed his broken family. Honestly, his son was super cute, but my true motivation was popcorn and milk duds.

When we got to the theater, his son wanted me to sit in the middle. I happily obliged. I could tell Bob's heart was swelling with pride. We nestled into our seats. About halfway through the movie, his little boy laid his head on my shoulder. Oh, how precious! He was going to take a nap on me! Kids seriously love me! I definitely need to pop a couple of these things out!

I snuggled back into my seat. Maybe this could actually work out. Holy crap. Maybe, I could totally fall in love with Bob and raise some feral little Jewish surfers. And just then, I felt it...

A little tiny hand slowly creeping across my T-shirt, making its way along my tummy, and heading further north. I adjusted myself. The little hand froze. A minute later it was back. OMG. This kid was totally trying to feel me up. Bob was completely engrossed in the movie and entirely oblivious to the fact that his first grader was attempting to molest me. I readjusted myself, carefully took his sticky little hand, and moved it away from my boob.

I sat there frozen for the rest of the movie. My bosom stood at full attention like the Queen's Guard on coronation day. I had no idea what to do. I didn't want to get his kid in trouble for attempting to steal second base. He was just a curious little boy. But I also didn't feel I was being unreasonable in my desire to not be molested. It is just personal preference.

I ultimately decided to handle it in the most mature way possible, a technique that I often suggest to my patients: avoidance. A few nights later, when Bob called me with a work emergency and asked if I could babysit, I quickly told him I had diarrhea. This was followed by a series of other miscellaneous, awkward excuses until I eventually moved back to California. I never told Bob what happened. I still haven't.

Looking back on that day, I wish I had handled it all so differently. In my defense, nobody teaches us how to handle these kinds of things. It's not common practice for grown adults to be felt up by six year olds. In hindsight, I do wish I had told Bob about the incident since boundaries are essential to healthy development. Of course, we all know that kids play "doctor," but usually their "patients" are a bit closer to their generation. To this day, I still feel like a coward for not addressing the issue.

Even though Bob and I didn't end up being a romantic fit, we had fun together. I had been through enough relationships to know that the physical aspects were not nearly as important as being with someone with solid character and a positive outlook on life. Bob fed the Bohemian, laissez faire part of my spirit and reminded me that good men do exist. Oh and I have it on good authority that Bob's son grew up to be well-adjusted and is thriving academically and athletically. My jury is still out on whether or not I will breastfeed. Oh and don't worry, I don't really recommend avoidance to my patients (just to my friends).

Child Molester Bob (or his six-year-old son)—not my person.

Take It From Me…
- Nice guys really do win most of the time.
- Movie popcorn is good, but totally not worth getting molested over.

Jungle Cat Bob

I met Jungle Cat Bob online just before my thirtieth birthday, when I was living in Minnesota for my doctoral residency program. Apparently this dude had invented some sort of horse racing product and was legit rolling in dough. Bob was divorced, had no children, and lived in a mansion on the ocean that had previously belonged to a professional athlete. We exchanged a few emails before we began talking on the phone.

Bob asked me what I wanted to do for my big 3-0. I told him I wanted to have my closest girlfriends all together somewhere. And just like that, Jungle Cat Bob invited me and up to six of my girlfriends to come celebrate my birthday at his mansion in South Beach. Conveniently, my mom was in Naples visiting her sister, so I decided to double down on my birthday festivities and have a little pre-birthday celebration with the family. Since this was during the time in my life when I refused to fly, I decided to take the train from Minnesota to Florida to go meet the fam and then Bob.

Mom and I road-tripped from Naples to Orlando and hit up all the Disney theme parks. While we were on our way to Disney World, I received a super disturbing call from Bob. He informed me that his ex-wife had killed herself that week and two days later, his father had died. I felt terrible for him and told him that we would just reschedule for another time. Bob was absolutely adamant that we keep my birthday plans. I was a little hesitant, but he convinced me that he was doing okay and that he welcomed a distraction from all that had occurred.

The next day, my mom and I decided to drive by Bob's house before checking into the beachfront hotel Bob got us for a couple days. Holy. Shit. This dude was seriously loaded. I dropped my mom back off at our hotel and headed straight to a salon to get a blowout and my nails done. I wanted to look like a million bucks considering his place was worth at least twenty million!

When I showed up at Bob's house, he was shorter than I expected. Like, he was definitely tall enough to ride Space Mountain, but I wasn't really physically attracted to him. Bob was a nice enough guy; he was obviously very intelligent and it was easy to be attracted to all the opulence that surrounded me. But when I kissed him, I felt absolutely zero connection. And I don't think Bob was into me either. After the uneventful kiss, Bob showed me around and we went to sit on some lounge chairs outside by his pool. I could tell he wasn't really there. Clearly, the shock of the week's traumatic events was in full effect. Bob was a total mess.

By the time my girlfriends showed up the next day, Bob somehow managed to pull himself together. He had thoughtfully hired a chef and a photographer for us. We spent the next couple days lounging by the pool, going out on his speed boat, riding jet skis, and having a private professional photo shoot. We drank and ate amazing food. This lifestyle clearly suited me. Maybe I could try hypnosis to see if I could force myself to fall in love with Bob.

Bob woke up and went to the gym every morning. He invited us to go, but I don't really do the whole "exercise thing," especially on vacation. My friend Jana, however, is totally ripped. The sister actually derives pleasure from voluntarily sweating. I know. Soooo weird, but I pride myself on being tolerant of people's bizarre quirks. I was like, "Bye Freaks" and rolled over and went back to sleep.

When they got back, Jana was laughing super hard. She told me that Bob had stopped at his dealer's house in his Ferrari to buy some Colombian bam bam before they went to the gym. Bob then proceeded to slam a protein shake (that was probably filled with human growth hormones) and went to hit the weights. We both just shrugged and went back to sipping our Skinny Girl daiquiris.

That night, while the girls and I went out to dinner and a club, Bob opted to stay home. We partied late into the night and then quietly retreated to our bedrooms in the mansion. Jana had volunteered to stay alone in the guest house. During the night we all heard someone trying to open our doors, but they were locked and we were too hungover to get up to see who was there.

A few hours later I heard a pounding on my door. I got up and found Jana standing there all pissed off, hand on hip. Apparently, after Bob tried to get into all of our bedrooms, he made his way into the guest house. Jana woke up at 5 am to some hazy little figure stripping down until he was in a cheetah print speedo.

Jana pulled the covers up tight around her and then watched as he started to seductively climb up onto her bed like a fucking jungle cat with a "come hither" look on his face. Except it was like a jungle cat who had just been sniffing some Bolivian Marching Powder. Dude was high as a mother fucking kite from his nose candy. He purred, "Heeeey you....Meow" and made claws out of his little hands. Jana squinted her eyes and nonchalantly said, "Oh, Hi Bob."

Bob tried to be all sexy even though he was totally coked out. He said, "I bet you like it rough, don't you?" Jana sighed and rolled her eyes. He continued, "What do you like? Puuuurrrrr." Jana flatly quipped, "Honestly Bob, I like choking men out in Jujitsu. I do it all the time. My boyfriend loves it."

Bob stopped for a second and then asked, "So that's a no?" Jana firmly nodded, "A definite 'no'. See you later, Bob." Bob slunk off the bed in his little tiny speedo and crawled out of the room. Bob was asleep when we left, so we wrote him a lovely thank you note and took off.

Jungle Cat Bob—not my person.

Take It From Me…

- Never believe anyone if they tell you they are "okay" following two deaths of loved ones.
- Being rich helps; being short doesn't.
- You can't force chemistry.
- The notion that people with tremendous wealth "have it easy" is not true. People are people. We all go through things.

Viper Bob

The very first time I saw Viper Bob was on a dating app. He was a decent looking guy—tall, successful, divorced, twelve years older than me, father of a young son, with a penchant for those expensive paisley-swirling "Robert Graham" shirts, blah blah blah. We chatted a bit online, but nothing ever transpired from our initial email interaction.

Fast forward a couple months: I was bartending at my super wealthy friend's Halloween party in Laguna Niguel to support my habit of getting college degrees. I had talked Jana, another poor grad student friend of mine, into working with me because I am not stingy and I owed her one for putting up with Jungle Cat Bob's antics. (Annnnd it is way more entertaining to make fun of rich people dressed like slutty pirates with someone.)

I was pouring wine, telling people how much I loved their dumb cat whiskers, when I noticed a man dressed up like a navy sailor staring at me. He looked familiar, but I knew I had never let his submarine penetrate me. I asked Jana for confirmation. "Oh yeah, he definitely wants to put his seamen in you, he's obviously rich, and he's not ugly...." I nodded in agreement and decided to lock it in.

By the end of the night, the sailor and I had exchanged numbers. A few days later, he showed up in a shiny red convertible Viper with a personalized license plate that read: "NW U LK ME" to pick me up for our first date. It all clicked when I saw his starched paisley covered shirt. Viper Bob and I laughed at our chance meeting. Bob had put the pieces together before picking me up, re-read my online profile with a list of my favorite things, and brought a box of my favorite See's Candies with him. Veeeery smooth. Obviously, the stars had aligned and the Universe was bringing us together. I had no idea how he was going to wedge a car seat into his sports car, but we had nine months to hash out the details.

A couple weeks later, Bob and I went to Las Vegas for the weekend. He wanted to get a suite overlooking the strip, but I insisted on two rooms because I am a woman of great virtue and also the proud owner of a disease-free vagina. We had a great time until I realized Bob was not just addicted to starched shirts with swirls, but also gambling. I watched as he parked himself at the high roller table, smack-dab in the middle of a bunch of billionaire Asians.

As I watched Bob throw thousands of dollars onto the poker table, I experienced what I am assuming was a moderate case of vertigo. The casino sounds became louder and louder and all the blinking lights felt as though they were caving in on me. To see my date tossing $500 chips on the table was positively unnerving to me. At least when men are blowing money on strippers, they will definitely get some boobies out of the deal and somebody will pretend to like them. Gambling offers no guarantee.

At one point, I closed my eyes and rubbed my temples as he threw at least two more student loans I could be paying off onto the table. My inner Jewish Mom instincts kicked in and I snagged a few chips from him so we could afford to get home just in case he was bluffing about having money. This proved to be unnecessary, Bob made an insane amount of money importing and exporting precious metals (or drugs) to other countries. I just wanted to ensure we had something to use as collateral should the mafia get involved.

Our second night in Vegas, Bob told me he was falling in love with me. Because Bob and I shared a handful of mutual acquaintances, I had done a little research. I would never take off for the weekend with a stranger. (Okay. That is a lie. I have totally done that. But I learned my lesson from Hurricane Bob.)

Word on the street was that Bob's penis got plenty of cardiovascular exercise. I am sure his professing of love on date five worked well for him in the past, however, he had finally met a worthy opponent to his pillow talk. I take great pride in my vagina and in fact, save all my A+ pap smear letters from my gynecologist to show my children one day. I was not having sex with him.

Paisley and poker addiction aside, Bob was unquestionably sweet and romantic. He was constantly lavishing me with compliments, thoughtful gifts, and even had a garden built to grow only purple roses when he learned they were my favorite flowers. I liked him, but I wasn't ready to pledge my undying love regardless of what his license plate was instructing me to do.

A few weeks after we went to Las Vegas, Bob and I went wine tasting in Temecula with my friend, Jana, and her boyfriend, Jeff. Bob rented a limo and we went to several fancy wineries. The four of us had a wonderful time getting what I like to call "classy-drunk" together. We were on such a high from the perfect day together that we cracked open a couple bottles and drank them on the ride home. On occasion, alcohol has caused me to fall in love with men; I was secretly hoping it would have the same effect on me with Bob.

Our limo driver pulled into my driveway and the four of us staggered out and into my house. We were starving, but I don't do the whole "grocery shopping" thing. It's hilarious to me when people tell me how lucky I am to stay in good shape despite not working out. Luck has nothing to do with it, people. As any proper Orange County girl will attest, it takes serious discipline and mind control to live off of cigarettes, a single package of tortillas, and coffee. This is made particularly challenging when your religious background includes food worship.

The most sober of the lot, Bob and Jana decided they would make a Del Taco run for all of us. I stayed with Jeff because Jana had serious plans to marry and breed with this man and she wanted to know if he felt the same way about her. As soon as Jana and Bob left, I went to town getting the 411 from Jeff.

Was he dating anyone else? Was he falling in love with Jana? Did he believe in marriage? How did he feel about kids? I was so committed to my gumshoe role that I lost track of time. When I checked my phone, I realized Jana and Bob had been gone for nearly an hour. I also realized I had ten missed calls from Jana, including a text that read in all caps: "I AM SO UNCOMFORTABLE!"

Just then, Bob and Jana pulled up and brought in the food. Jana had a strange, semi-traumatized look to her. She pulled me aside and informed me that Bob had repeatedly hit on her and even attempted to kiss her in the drive-thru. I stood there in total shock, knowing full-well she was telling me the truth. Jana begged me not to mention anything to Jeff because he would go ballistic.

I grabbed Bob, pulled him outside and asked him what the fuck was wrong with him. Bob told me to "give him a break

74

since I was all over Jeff in the limo." I was absolutely floored and appalled by his accusation. This could not be further from the truth as I was unquestionably the biggest cheerleader of Jana and Jeff. I called a cab and made Bob leave immediately. I was so distraught; I couldn't even eat my veggie burrito, and I love Del Taco.

For many weeks after, Bob would call me, tell me how much he missed me, and literally beg for another chance. He sent me flowers and pictures of the rose garden. I remember feeling so disheartened about dating someone who was so incredibly doting and yet, had still tried to cheat on me. If you can't trust the motives of a man who consistently demonstrates adoration and is seemingly so smitten with you, who can you trust? Dating can make you feel like you are going fucking crazy!

This experience was really troubling for me, and not just because Bob tried to make-out with my best friend (which is always completely taboo). I wasn't in love with Bob, but I wanted to be. I was giving this relationship a legitimate opportunity to flourish.

Bob treated me like a priority, he shared his excitement about a future, and he even had me spend time with his six-year-old son on multiple occasions. When he betrayed me, I began to deeply question my intuition. I think the worst part of betrayal is how it causes you to question your own instincts: "Why did I trust him?" and "How did I not see this coming?" Despite Viper Bob's incessant phone calls and attempts at redemption, I never went back to him. The trust was broken, and something inside me told me I would not get it back.

Bob and I lived in the same part of town and traveled in some of the same social circles, so I would occasionally run into him at various events and parties. Every time, he was with a new woman. Always beautiful, busty, and usually half-dressed. These women seemed more like trophies than actual partners. It became all too obvious that Bob was overcompensating for some serious self-worth issues. His M.O. for numbing his feelings of inadequacy was to gamble, keep a revolving door of women on speed dial, zip around in expensive cars, and of course clad himself in those goddamn expensive swirly starched shirts. Bob was a lost person, programmed by a world that has taught men their self-worth is dependent upon their possessions.

The saddest part of it all is that there was another side to Bob. In rare, precious glimpses, I was able to see him for who he truly was under the phony exterior. Bob was a sensitive, gentle soul who grew up in a close-knit family on a farm in Iowa. He had a real kindness and vulnerability that longed to be freely expressed and accepted. Instead, he chose to suppress this person with countless vices. Ironically, the suppressed Bob was the person I could have fallen in love with, because this person was real. I was hit with the stark realization that just because Bob was in his forties, he really had no clue who he was.

I ran into Bob at yet another Halloween party a few years later. To my amazement, he was alone—no bombshell hanging on his arm. I, on the other hand, was on a date. Without notice, Bob pulled my date aside and told him how lucky he was to be with me. He told him to "never let me go" and that I "was the most incredible woman he had ever met." I would like to think that deep down, Bob knew I had caught a glimpse of his wholeness and authentic self in the months we were together. And like all of us, what Bob really wanted was to be accepted and loved for who he truly was. (Yes. This is now the second time a dude I was dating hit on Jana. Yes. I should probably send her a gift card to Chipotle or some shit. Girl is a true sistah.)

Viper Bob—not my person.

Take It From Me...
- Pay attention to personalized license plates as they are extremely telling.
- If your boyfriend hits on your friend, this is an automatic ejection from the game.
- Expensive starched swirly shirts are lame.

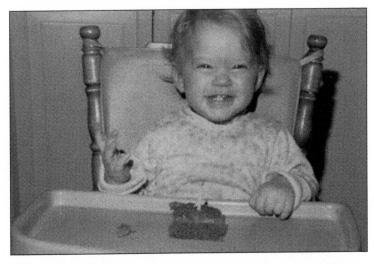

My first birthday. I wasn't gluten, dairy, meat, or sugar free yet.

My first Passover;
I told you I was Jewish.

Dad making my peanut M&M costume.

I was not kidding about being a hardcore tomboy.

Softball was no laughing matter.

Ph.D Ceremony

Me and Jana in the limo mid-winetasting with her future-husband and Viper Bob.

Paramount Oscar Party

Just hanging with Liam Neeson on set. Ho hum....

Who wore it better?

My first public manifesto.

My first photo shoot.

Already taking the world by the balls.

Taking a night off from Toddler Bob and enjoying a Nuggets game with Laurinda.

Still trying to get Bub to convert.

Me and Mom

*Lake Havasu on Dad's boat with Becky right before
Counterfeit Cop Bob made his entrance.*

*One of the many times Mom let me ditch school
to go to Disneyland.*

"Hey, Erin! We really did it!"

*Other than the time of the "incident,"
Foul Ball Bob and I had a great time
together.*

85

Home sweet home with Bub.

*My birthday dinner with Kathy during the
El Diablo Bob fiasco.*

My first beauty pageant.

*Me and Bub celebrating our birthdays together
for the first time.*

Bub and I crashed Mom & Dad's birthday trip to Graceland.

Me and Carol at a pre-production event for one of the TV pilots Director Bob and I created.

Keeping it classy at age 19.   *I took modeling very seriously.*

""""What did you do today?""""
"""Wrote a book with you.""""
High Five."

Just taking in this crazy, beautiful, wonderful life.

Director Bob

"**Y**ou are perfect to remind my brother of the contours of a woman."

I stared at the man who said this to me with expectant eyes. "Well, where is your brother? Tell him to come down!" I was on a business trip in San Francisco and having a drink with my friend Lisa at the hotel bar.

The man smiled and said, "He is in Tennessee."

I groaned.

"He is going through a messy divorce, but you two are supposed to meet. He is a director and recently won an award at Cannes. I am going to give you his email."

I rolled my eyes and groaned again.

I spent a few more minutes chatting with the man who had a mysterious brother. He informed me that he was in San Francisco on business, married with children, and the vice president of some major company. I told him I was a business coach and this was why I was in San Francisco working that weekend. He told me he was potentially interested in hiring me. I gave him my information and said goodbye. As I was leaving, he whispered his room number in my ear. I just condescendingly patted him on the shoulder and said, "Okay, buddy." Lisa and I laughed at the sheer absurdity of the situation. "You should totally date my brother, but I want to bone you first!" Eew.

I was admittedly surprised when I received an email from his brother, Director Bob. We began regularly corresponding with one another. It wasn't long before I decided I was entirely captivated by this man. Our conversations quickly became deep and thought-provoking. I felt inexplicably drawn to him. Two months passed before Bob informed me he was flying out to L.A. with his niece who had a movie audition. He asked if I would I like to meet. I nervously and excitedly replied yes.

I booked a room at the same hotel Bob and his niece would be staying at. We met in the downstairs lobby after his niece went to bed. Bob was from Brazil, wore thick artsy glasses, had a scarf wrapped loosely around his neck, and was like nobody I had ever seen before. I had never been more instantly entranced by another human being. It was as though my soul had finally discovered what she desperately longed for.

We were immediately taken with one another. Our conversation had an impenetrable depth and insight for two people who had just met. We sat side by side drinking red wine, reading poetry. We were completely mesmerized by one another's presence, utterly oblivious to anyone around us. It was as though a cosmic collision had occurred.

Bob walked me up to my room, where I slipped into the bathroom and put on a pair of baby pink valor pajamas to be more comfortable. Lie. I totally did this on purpose. I wanted him to get a better view of my goods. I was totally going for the "I am not even trying and I look this hot look," even though I was obviously trying.

Bob stared at me in a way that made my knees go weak. He murmured, "Your body is so beautiful." We laid on the bed and kissed. Electricity shot through me. And apparently his as well because he had an immediate and sizable boner. OMG. Pinch me. Was this for real? Who was this man? He was brilliant, soulful, a great kisser, AND he had a big penis?

We pried ourselves apart and I laid awake thinking about him for hours until I eventually drifted off to sleep. The next morning, I was woken by a loud knock on the door. I fucking loathe waking up early. I could probably sleep through an appendectomy sans anesthesia if it was scheduled before noon. I yelled at housekeeping that I was dead and to come back later. The knocking continued. I rolled out of bed and stumbled to the door feeling dangerously stabby.

I opened the door, and there was Bob standing in the doorway. My mood instantly lightened. "Good morning. I am leaving for the studio, but I had to make sure you were real." My knees went weak. I was so taken by him that I momentarily forgot I have OCD and spend fifteen minutes a day brushing and flossing my teeth every morning and then again at night. I leaned in and kissed him...with morning breath.

Later that day, I had lunch with my mom. She teasingly asked how my date went the night before. My family knows my "good date: date" ratio, and likely surmised this was another failed attempt at finding love. I casually announced, "I'm pretty sure I met my soulmate." My mom dropped her fork mid-bite because she knew how many dates I had been on in search of my person, and I had never once uttered these words.

After Bob returned to Tennessee, we would talk, text, and Skype every single day. A couple of weeks went by before Bob began flying out every other weekend to see me. We were absolutely smitten. I introduced him to my family, we went out to eat, drank good wine, stayed up all night talking, made love to each other, and we began shooting little videos together. (Calm down, Dad, not sex ones.) Finally, I was being given permission to stoke the flame of creativity within me that had longed to be expressed. Bob thought I had actual talent to be an actor, and this was the validation I had been desperately seeking.

At the time, I was working on my doctorate and was in the midst of writing my dissertation. Since I could theoretically complete this anywhere, Bob and I decided that I should come out to Tennessee for a while to live with him and his three children. He purchased a one-way ticket for me and a round-trip ticket for my mom so she could accompany my flight-phobic ass on the plane. I was desperately afraid to fly, but missing him was even harder. I packed up my belongings and boarded a plane.

Bob picked up me and my mom from the airport and brought us to his beautiful, contemporary home, tucked away in the mountains of the "Country Music Capital of the World." So awesome. Honestly, it would have probably been cooler to live in the "Rap Capital" or even the "Smooth Jazz Capital," but whatevs.

We met his darling children and became acquainted in what would be my new home. I tilted my head and exchanged a glance with my mom as we discovered a large picture of his ex-wife hanging in the stairwell. I was probably just being paranoid. He was obviously doing this for the kids. She had cheated on him. He couldn't possibly still have feelings for her. Right? Regardless, I decided I would hire an artist to paint a nude portrait of me draped on a chaise lounge with a full bush. I started laughing. Bob was going to love it.

The next day Bob had to go to work. He left my mom and I to watch the kids. We took them shopping and to an arcade. My very sweet and proper mom was unimpressed that Bob did not leave us any money to entertain his children. It wasn't that we needed money, it was simply the principal behind it. I just shrugged it off, maybe he had simply forgotten or maaaaaybe Bob was going to convert to Judaism!

A few days later, my mom returned home and Bob and I went on our first "real date" in my new town. We walked into a restaurant and everyone was staring at us. It occurred to me that Bob was somewhat of a celebrity in this town, and I was the new woman on his arm. While I felt flattered by the attention, I sensed that Bob was uncomfortable. We sat side by side, having a romantic dinner when Bob suddenly became quite abrasive and short. I quietly said, "You feel like ice to me right now." He had gone from being so loving and romantic to someone entirely foreign to me. He offered nothing other than he was "tired."

We drove home in deafening silence. I never found out what had made Bob so angry that night. I do remember calling my friend Carol from the backyard the next morning and telling her I thought I should come home. She told me not to make any rash decisions. I shrugged off my feelings of uneasiness, walked back inside, and completely enveloped myself in my new life.

I began to build a bond with the children and spent a lot of time with them. I took them shopping, attended science fairs, played games, and helped with their homework. When I wasn't working on my dissertation or occupied with the kids, I began working on the genesis of Bob's new film projects. At first, Bob seemed to welcome my ideas and would take me to shoots with him. I had always wanted to pursue my creative side, but never knew how to get started; this was a game-changer (actually, a life-changer) for me.

One day Bob's former wife came over. Bob's ex was an actress and producer. They were wrapping up a project they had been working on together. She dismissively said hi to me as she breezed past into what was now my kitchen. I felt uncomfortable with the exchange. I went in the other room and sat down in one of his peculiar, ultra-contemporary chairs to work on my dissertation and give them privacy. At one point, I stood up and walked into the kitchen as she was leaning over to take a bite of Bob's burrito off his plate. What the hell was that about? Your ex does not eat your burrito once you are finito. It's a law. Google it.

Bob assured me he was definitely "over her." Several weeks later, his ex-wife invited me to tea. The kids were obviously talking about me, and I think Burrito Eater realized I was there to stay. We spent three hours talking. She told me about her marriage to Bob. She was candid in her admission to having affairs. She informed me that she and Bob's sex life was "non-existent."

I was admittedly surprised because Bob and I had an incredible sex life. In fact, it was the most intense love-making I had ever experienced. We could never get enough of each other. I had never craved the touch of man like I did his. Not only was this man brilliant (like do the *New York Times* crosswords in PEN while on the potty brilliant), but he also represented to me the possibly of my heart *and* my creativity finding a home. I was in deep.

Life carried on and Bob continued to champion my creativity. He made me promises that I would become the producer while he would remain the director of his projects. I drastically cut my number of coaching clients so I could focus on making films with Bob. It felt so exhilarating to be receiving validation for my creative abilities rather than just my intelligence and athleticism. Bob gave me the courage to change my name to keep my "doctor world" separate from my acting world. I selected the last name of Kleine to pay homage to my doctoral mentor who had passed away only months prior.

In the midst of all these amazing transformations, I also began to notice a subtle competitive energy coming from Bob. He would coldly dismiss my ideas without really listening. Promises fell by the wayside. He became distant, work would take precedence, and I often felt as though I was in the way. Most of the time, I would bite my tongue, keep my ideas to myself, and do what I could to take up less space. When I would attempt to express my concerns, he would soothe my mounting insecurities by once again saying, "It's just going to take me time to believe you are real."

I was thrilled when Bob was invited to give a presentation to a bunch of celebs, movers and shakers, and high-profile Hollywood executives. I accompanied him and tried to mollify his nerves, to no avail. Five minutes before show time, I pulled out all the stops, unbuttoned his pants in his dressing room, and gave him the best blow job of his life. Like, I deserved an Oscar for "Best Supporting Girlfriend." Bob proceeded to go on stage and absolutely crush it…thanks to me.

We returned home and began working on a TV pilot together, but jealousy began creeping in and leaving its ugly stain. Bob would accuse me of having affairs. He even accused me of cheating on him with women. I would remind him that I have never been on a hike in my life and that I wouldn't be caught dead in those hybrid zipper pant-shorts that my lesbian friends wear. I vacillated between anger and reassuring him how much I loved him and how devoted I was to our relationship and our projects. And again, his infamous line—"I just can't believe you are real"—would keep me on the hook.

At the time, Bob and I were working on a project that required us to raise capital before we could pitch it to Hollywood executives. I immediately sprung into action and asked my long-standing coaching clients to invest in us. This came with a daunting sense of responsibility, as I desperately wanted to pay them back and make them proud. As fate would have it, the show didn't sell and this would prove to be the first of many blows to come. And I am not talking about the kind I gave him before his speech to a bunch of famous people.

One night right before Thanksgiving, Bob left his computer open and I decided to snoop. I clicked on an open tab and stood there shaking in disbelief. Bob was having affairs (as in plural) with women online. My brain struggled to make sense of what I was reading. No. No, this couldn't be. I felt a wave of nausea rising. I swallowed hard. Please God, No. Not him. I love him. There must be some explanation. This was a misunderstanding. But it was very much real. Bob had plans in motion to meet with one of the women he was communicating with. I felt as though I had been gutted as the words meshed together on the screen. I reached down and placed my hand on the desk to steady myself.

I became completely unhinged in a way I had never experienced before. I tore up the stairs to confront him, blinded by my tears of devastated fury. I went absolutely ballistic—screaming, crying, and shaking. I was inconsolable. I punched him in the chest. He was pleading with me to let him explain. I finally collapsed onto my knees in utter shock and disbelief. Bob tried to calm me down. He justified the affairs by saying nothing had ever happened. He said they were just harmless and flattering for his ego. I was numb with grief. I quickly made plans to go spend Thanksgiving with my good friend Robert and his boyfriend in Chicago.

My mind replayed all the times Bob would accuse me of things that had never happened. I remembered when I had gone home to see my parents and he had called and cruelly ended our relationship over the affairs he assumed I was having that actually did not exist. I had hysterically called him back over and over again only to have my calls go to voicemail. I vividly remember sitting in a parking lot in Laguna Niguel pounding on my steering wheel, contemplating ending my life because I hurt so badly.

I felt sick as I realized all the crazy accusations Bob had made were actually him projecting his own fears, jealousy, and guilt onto me. He was demolished when his ex-wife had cheated on him and yet, he began to make his own way down the road of infidelity. He knew what deep seeded pain this would cause. It didn't stop him.

Bob's paranoia, jealousy, and blatant disregard at times were completely illogical and would drive me to the brink of insanity. Then, in the wake of his destructive behavior, he would have a moment of clarity, and we would go back to a blissful romance. This relationship was by far the most bipolar relationship I have ever had. Finally, when my heart could not take any more of the broken promises, it officially ended. I wondered if I would ever feel whole again. I wondered if I would ever have this same connection with another person. I wondered if I would ever stop hurting. For me, Director Bob was the man I wanted to partner with in life. I took our talks of marriage, having a child, and making movies together seriously. I envisioned a future of complete partnership. When it ended, I felt my heart and my spirit break.

After leaving Bob's, I decided to go stay with my friend Jen in Atlanta until I figured out my next move. Bob drove me, and I cried most of that drive. I ended up living in Atlanta for four years. I spent two of those years getting over him. Bob was one of my greatest loves and heartbreaks and through this, I learned how strong of a woman I truly am. I also learned that although Bob thought he liked my independent and strong personality, when it came down to it, he wanted to be with a woman who was dependent on him—a woman who would allow him to run the show.

Through this relationship, I learned that I want a man to be a man, while also embracing my gifts. A man who does not feel like less of a man just because I am more of a woman. I want to freely express myself and speak up when I feel compelled, without this equating to some sort of threat to my partner's manhood or ego. During some of our worst fights, Bob would say, "There can only be one captain." This declaration never resonated with me. It felt like a paradigm riddled with power struggle and too contractual for me. I want a hierarchy-free partnership where we flow and can take turns steering the ship.

Director Bob—an instrumental person in my life, but not my person.

Take It From Me...
- Don't quit your day job.
- If the ex is still hanging in the hallway and eating your burritos, not enough time has passed.
- Pay attention to the creepy brother.
- You cannot make someone trust you if they are not ready to trust.
- Never make yourself small just to make someone else more comfortable.
- We have multiple soulmates.
- We can survive heartbreak.
- Country music is not so bad after all.

Katy Perry Bob

Katy Perry Bob and I met for dinner at a trendy restaurant in Atlanta before attending a Katy Perry concert together. I was pleasantly surprised and relieved that he looked like his online photos. So many people bullshit their profiles, lying about their age, height, and posting ancient photos of what they used to look like, usually twenty pounds thinner and with several thousand more hair strands on their head.

Bob seemed like a nice, wholesome, easy-going man who I could possibly settle down with in the burbs and live out the dream. Physically, Katy Perry Bob was classically handsome, yet he also reminded me of a caricature. His face was oddly exaggerated in certain areas and it almost looked like he was wearing makeup. It's not that he was unfortunate looking, but I would obviously prefer if our children had more (all) of my features. I decided I could still love the kids if they bore slight resemblance to him. And besides, it was far more important to me that his moral character was intact.

Katy Perry Bob proved to be both charismatic and considerate as he opened every door for me and gave me his coat when he noticed I was cold. He thoughtfully called an Uber to take us to the concert two blocks away so I wouldn't have to walk in my heels. He patiently waited in the merchandise line for a half an hour with me and then bought me a "California Dreams" t-shirt. For a first date, I was having a really fun time! Who knows, this might be the one! I could simply refer him to a better plastic surgeon once his filler wore off, and things could be perfect between us.

We were dancing and singing along to Katy Perry (she is such a bad-ass!) when he randomly looked down at his phone and realized he had a bunch of missed calls. He excused himself and returned maaaaybe three minutes later. I asked him if everything was okay. He yelled over the music, "OH YEAH, MY MOM JUST DIED!" I choked on my beer and screamed back, "OMG! I AM SO SORRY! LET ME GRAB MY PURSE AND WE CAN GO!" He put his hand on my arm and yelled back into my ear, "OH NO, NO! IT'S FINE! SERIOUSLY! THESE TICKETS WERE EXPENSIVE!" WTF. I stood there stunned silent while Bob resumed dancing.

I understood it was too late and his mother wasn't going to get any dead"er", but I am Jewish. We fucking *live* for death. We have traditions, rituals, and customs and then when those are finished, we have even more traditions, rituals, and customs to commiserate our loved, and even our hated, ones. Then we still have parties YEARS later to further honor their prior existence. It. Is. Just. What. We. Do.

The concert ended and we took an Uber back to the restaurant where we had left our cars. Katy Perry Bob was in a jovial mood, chatting away. My shrink brain was searching through every file system trying to justify his unsettling behavior. Everyone grieves differently, and I finally decided Katy Perry Bob was simply in shock and the gravity of the situation would soon hit him. So, being the selfless fount of altruism that I am, I decided I would follow him back to his place to ensure he was okay.

I discovered that Katy Perry Bob lived downtown in an insanely nice, swanky loft. He immediately made a beeline for the wine, where he selected an expensive red and poured us each a glass. He then opened a bottle of chilled champagne that he had "been saving for a special occasion." I was now convinced his poor dead mother must have been a crack whore. Like a really mean, terrible, evil crack whore with a controlling pimp. I mean, you don't get this way just because your mom selfishly chose to formula feed your ass to spare her nice rack. How else could you explain this detached, emotionally barren soul? He made a toast to his mother while I said some silent prayers in Hebrew.

At this point, I expected to bear witness to an emotional breakdown of sorts. Instead, Katy Perry Bob turned on some sexy music and pushed a button to light his fireplace. My eyes darted back and forth. OMG. His mom wasn't even cold yet and he was more concerned about the ambiance. My vagina was legit dryer than an Arizona desert in August. Katy Perry Bob leaned over to kiss me. I slithered out from underneath him. "Look, Bob—I had a wonderful evening, but I am tired and I know you must be just beside yourself. Lots of stuff for you to process and work through...I am just going to leave now."

"No! I am great! Stay!" He patted the couch next to him. "Seriously, we are all going to die!"

Thanks, dipshit, I had no idea. I watch enough Dateline to know this was the type of dude who was going to turn me into a lampshade. Not tonight, pal. I quickly dropped a few strands of hair to assist the prosecuting attorney in case I actually did go missing, and bolted for the door.

*A week later, I saw Bob's mother's obituary on his social media page. She was not a crack whore after all. She was a piano teacher for the elderly and loved by everyone. Everyone except her one rogue psycho son. God Bless her soul.

Katy Perry Bob—not my person.

Take It From Me...

- If a man has this little of an emotional connection to his own mother, it's pretty certain he will never be able to emotionally connect with you.

- As we move through life, we will all experience loss. While everyone handles loss differently, it is helpful to be with someone whose grieving process is at least on the same planet as yours.

- Katy Perry is fabulous live!

Lebanese Bob

I met Lebanese Bob online shortly after I had moved to Atlanta to grieve my relationship with Director Bob. I was still reeling from my most recent heartbreak and was hesitant to get involved with someone again. And if Katy Perry Bob was a good indicator of the men out there, I was in no hurry to hitch my wagon. Lebanese Bob was persistent though, and I eventually caved and agreed to go out with him.

Bob knew I was an actress and took me to some Shakespearean play for our first date. It was boring as fuck, and I was desperately trying to stay awake. *If you suffer from insomnia, I strongly encourage you to attend one of these performances. I was just about to tell old Bob that I had a sudden bout of diarrhea or rush the stage and drink some of Juliet's poison, when he leaned over and asked if I wanted to get out of there. Hmmm…Bob was perceptive. This might work out after all…

Bob was definitely different than anyone I had ever dated before. He had immigrated to America from Lebanon when he was nineteen, and his was a true "rags to riches" story. He had come to the United States with no money, unable to speak English, and with no friends. After moving in with an uncle he barely knew, he worked incredibly hard to achieve the "American Dream" and eventually ended up being hugely successful in the fine art industry. Bob had made a very nice life for himself. He was polite, kind, never arrogant, and extremely generous. On our second date he gave me $2,000 Tiffany necklace.

It felt good to be wanted and pursued so strongly again after my last relationship. More than anything, it felt good to be with a man who appeared to genuinely like my larger than life, trail-blazin' personality. I had decided to be completely honest about everything I had accomplished thus far and the things I was still working on. I would no longer minimize myself to make a man feel more comfortable being with me. Bob seemed entirely un-daunted and even excited for everything I had already achieved and the things I was hoping to create in my life.

I learned that Bob had been in a relationship for three years with a woman who was twelve years older than him in Washington, D.C., but that had eventually fizzled out. Bob was three years my junior, so obviously that cougar had mauled him. We began to see one another more frequently. Bob invested in my company at the time and refused to call it a loan. He simply wanted me to flourish and not be stressed out over money. He lavished me with gifts and fun dates, sans Shakespeare. Even though I was renting a place not far from his, we were basically living together in his townhouse.

I eventually decided to bring Bob home to meet my ultra-conservative parents for the holidays. I was admittedly more ner-vous for this introduction than I was to fly on an airplane. Bob was compassionate about my flying phobia and rented a car to drive us from Atlanta to California. Before Bob and I hit the road, I gave my parents a highlight reel of information about my new foreign boy toy.

Along the way, we stayed at the nicest hotels, dined at expensive restaurants, and Bob proved to be a perfect gentleman. The man wouldn't even let me pick up my suitcase. We went to the opening night of 'Rent' in Austin and stayed in a beachside condo in San Diego. It was amazing…I didn't even feel like choking him out after spending seventy-two hours in the car together.

We eventually arrived at my parents' house, where my gigantic father wasted no time sitting Bob down and grilling him over the Koran for the next three hours. My dad doesn't have truck nuts or a confederate flag flying from the back of his pick-up, but the man is definitely an old school patriotic patriarch. Bob innocently informed my father that he was not a practicing Muslim, and that he identified himself as an atheist. I sighed and shook my head at Bob's naivety. Naturally, this prompted a whole new round of questioning regarding Bob's childhood since my dad clearly didn't believe him.

I was actually impressed by Bob's patience and cunning restraint with my father's personalized custom's department. After a couple days of intense interrogation and being the recipient of my dad's side eye, Bob flew home to return to work while I spent a week with my family. Before I left, my dad hugged me tightly, and reminded me how important it was for me to be with a man who loved God and this country.

I definitely wasn't in love with Bob, knowing that we lacked the soulful connection that I so desperately craved, but I was fond of him. I was happy to see him when I returned to Atlanta. Honestly, the only thing that I ever found to be annoying was when he would go get testosterone pellets in his ass and then proceed to act like a douche for the next few days. He could also be a little controlling at times and he definitely liked to be the "man of the house." But there was nothing that really stood out to suggest that Bob wasn't a stand-up guy—or so I thought…

Bob and I were invited to a beautiful vineyard that was hosting a "Roaring 20s" themed party for New Year's Eve. We both arrived dressed to the nines and ordered our drinks. We were socializing with the other guests as I sipped my chardonnay. We spent the evening dancing, chatting up new people, and tasting wine varietals. I had about three glasses of wine over the course of the night and felt a solid buzz as we rang in the new year.

Bob and I shared a glass of champagne before calling it quits and heading to our suite. The last thing I remember about that night was getting in the elevator and feeling like I went from nicely buzzed to a total drunk mess. I don't even remember getting into our room or undressing. There is a sizable chunk of time missing for me because the next moment I can recall, was waking up around 4am with my back throbbing and feeling super hungover.

The next morning, we drove home as I tried to piece together the evening's events. My back was still killing me and I could not rationalize how I became utterly hammered after less than four drinks in a seven-hour period. Back in the day, I could have put down four drinks in an hour and still been relatively functional. We stopped for brunch and talked about the party. Bob casually remarked, "Last night was my favorite time we ever had sex because you were so relaxed and let me do whatever I wanted to you."

I sat there in stunned silence. I DID NOT EVEN REMEMBER HAVING SEX WITH HIM. I was incredibly disturbed that Bob's "favorite" time to be intimate with me was when I was completely incapacitated. I felt myself detaching from this man as the trust I once had in him entirely evaporated in that moment. It slowly occurred to me that Bob selfishly enjoyed this moment because he had full control over me.

Our relationship began to deteriorate after this incident, not to mention my back was becoming increasingly more painful. Bob informed me he had to attend an art show in New York. I didn't think anything of it until I saw his phone and realized he had booked a flight to D.C.. When I confronted him, Bob told me he had been missing his ex and wanted to see her. He tried to assure me they were only friends, as if I would buy that! The dude straight-up lied to me about the trip and never would have told me if I had not seen the airline ticket on his phone. I had heard all this bullshit before. Why did this keep happening to me? I knew I deserved so much better and yet, here I was once again.

It didn't help that I soon discovered a supposed friend of mine was telling Bob things behind my back. Our relationship had reached a boiling point, and the night before my Ph.D. ceremony, Bob and I got into a huge fight. He told me I was "spoiled" and that he knew I was "never that into him." He went on to tell me that I was not the right girl for him because I was too independent and he wanted to be with a woman who made him feel needed. Here it was again, the same old pattern of a man falling hard and fast for me, but then deciding my ambition was too much, that I was too independent, and that I was not needy enough.

I was instantly gripped by my old fear once again; except this time, I was pissed. I was now in my thirties, and the cycle was still repeating itself. I was raised to be independent and to never have to rely on a man. But my being this way—my hard work, my achievements, the very things I wanted someone to be proud of—were scaring men off. I felt like I had done everything wrong. What was the point of accomplishing all that I had if I was just going to end up alone? I wanted to be with a man who was proud of everything I had done with my life. I wanted someone to love and champion me. I didn't want to have to make myself small anymore to compensate for their insecurities.

I packed up all my stuff and drove back to my place. I cried the entire night and was still crying the next morning when my parents arrived from California to attend my doctoral graduation. Here we were, at a time worthy of absolute celebration, and I couldn't stop sobbing. Ashamed at my latest failed attempt at love, I told my parents that Lebanese Bob and I had broken up. I figured this would elicit some joy from my father who was never really a fan of Bob's. Without any admonishment or condemnation in his voice, my dad said, "Stefanie, what you need to understand is that you have no blems...you are like a tire with no blems."

"A what?"

"When I was a kid and my friends and I wanted new tires for our cars, we would look for a tire with no blems. We would search for perfect tires. You have no blems. You have no baggage, no ex-husbands, no kids, and you have your head on straight. So, you need to remember that you deserve a tire with no blems too. You belong with a top-caliber man. Lebanese Bob is not right for you. Period."

Once again, I was reminded of where I came from and how much my parents love me. I pulled my shit together and walked across that stage blem-free, to collect my diploma. After thirteen years of education, I was officially a doctor. So yeah, add that to my list of intimidation factors, mother fuckers. Oh, and I wore my favorite blue bikini under my cap and gown, for everyone who graciously informed me I didn't look the part of a doctor. You were totally right!

As it turns out, Bob had been so rough with me the night at the vineyard, that he had actually herniated an injured disk in my back. For months afterwards, I sought physical therapy and spinal epidurals. Nothing was working, so I eventually opted to have surgery to repair the physical damage he had caused. I chose to never confront Bob over what he had done. Part of me felt responsible for becoming too intoxicated. Part of me wondered if he even knew I was blacked out.

The truth is, I never told anyone about that night. The logical side of my brain knew that what had happened was wrong. Surely a man I was living with for months, had to know I was not actively participating in the sex he was having with me that night. He had to know I was not really "there." On some level, he had to know he was taking advantage of me. If this had happened to one of my friends, I would be irate. But for some reason, aside from the initial shock I experienced when he told me we had sex on New Year's Eve, I never experienced the typical symptoms a victim of sexual violation experiences.

I realize now that there is not necessarily a linear path to follow in the wake of trauma. In this instance, for whatever reason, I was okay. I am absolutely not excusing his behavior. I am just saying that there is no right or wrong way to process trauma. The most important thing to do is honor how you feel about it and to give yourself the space and grace to heal in the way that best serves you.

Lebanese Bob—not my person.

Take It From Me...

- Do not ever have sex with an incapacitated human. I really shouldn't have to say that.
- It is okay to be okay after a trauma.
- There is no timeline to break a cycle or thought pattern.
- You are worthy of love.
- You should not have to be needy to be wanted.
- Do NOT buy tires with blems.

Toddler Bob

My mom is originally from Colorado, and my parents were considering moving back to the Mile High City from Orange County. We are a nomadic tribe and collectively decided to take a trip to the Rockies to see if this move felt right. I made plans to stay with my childhood friend, Laurinda, for a few weeks, while my parents stayed with my Aunt Shari. As we passed the 'Welcome to Colorado' sign, I decided to change my online dating profile to the Denver area juuuuuust in case someone spectacular was waiting for me there.

Well low and behold, I promptly received a message from a man we shall refer to as "Toddler Bob." His profile had the Italian quote, "Si vis amari, ama" which translates into "If you wish to be loved, love." Whatever. We made arrangements to meet at a swanky restaurant outside of Denver. I arrived before Bob and was sitting on a bench waiting when I felt a gust of wind. The next thing I knew, Bob came sliding up next to me and said, "Rosenberg Party of Two?!" I started laughing.

Bob was Jewish, funny, divorced with identical twin daughters, quick-witted, charming, Jewish, handsome, super tall (like

6'5", which is unheard of for Jewish men), blond and blue-eyed (also, rare for Jewish men), smart, charismatic, a gynecologist (so he could definitely locate my clitoris), and he was Jewish. Our waitress absolutely loved us and even commented about how much fun we were. Clearly, this was serendipitous; everything I had been through was leading up to this! Who knew I'd find my B'Shert (Jewish word for beloved) in Colorado? I totally thought I would have to take another pilgrimage to the Holy Land, or at least Manhattan.

Our food was brought out and the waitress came to check on us. Bob suddenly snapped at her, "THE FOOD IS FINE! WHAT DO YOU WANT ME TO SAY?" I thought he was joking with her and started to giggle. His face remained stone cold. Ummm… What in the ever-loving-fuck was that? Our waitress turned red and quickly left. Dinner resumed. Maybe he was just hangry? Like, I can be a little bitchy when I don't get my gluten-free, sugar-free, soy-free, vegetarian except for fish, with slightly overcooked salmon, salad with the dressing on the side. Dinner resumed and everything was fabulous.

Bob dropped me off at Laurinda's apartment and told me he had his daughters the next day. I thanked him for dinner and went inside to gush to my childhood friend about meeting Prince Charming and how I loved Colorado. The next morning, Bob sent me a text asking if he could bring me coffee. Um, yes, please. Ten minutes later, he showed up with Starbucks. A Jew that buys overpriced lattes. I likey… He told me he was taking his kids to an indoor trampoline place and invited me to come along. I felt a little uneasy about meeting his children the day after I had met him, but he assured me he would tell them we were just friends.

It suddenly occurred to me that Bob had taken note of my well-endowed rack. OF COURSE he wanted to watch me jump on a trampoline. This man was smart, I tell you. His twin girls were absolutely darling. One of the twins darted off to peg some weaker kids in the face at dodgeball while I jumped with the other one. We convinced Bob to come jump with us. His daughter was so happy because it was the first and only time Bob had ever jumped with her. Boobs are magical like that.

It was as though I had found my instant family and simply needed to add water. After the trampoline place, we went to get sushi. As we were parking, Bob turned to his young teenage daughters and said, "I spent $300 on dinner with Stefanie last night. I am telling you this so you know how you should be treated." And I totally didn't sleep with your dad because I am worth way more than $300 and so are you, young impressionable girls!

Bob took his kids home after dinner, tucked them in, and came back over to Laurinda's apartment complex where I was staying. We snuck into the yoga studio and talked for hours. Bob admitted that he had a vested interest in me moving here and that he would help me in any way I needed. I laid in bed that night thinking it was all going to be okay. My parents liked it here, I can make friends anywhere, I've already met a guy, and everything about this new adventure greatly appealed to my gypsy soul.

I could actually see Bob and I having a life together. A mature, family-centric life. A life where I could leave behind my superficial Southern California past. No more "who is prettier than who" and "who makes more money" nonsense. The thought immediately put me at ease since the need to inject my ass fat into my face would not be far off if I remained in the my-face-matters-more-than-my-soul Orange County. Besides, I had never really dated anyone who was Jewish before; maybe this was the missing link I was looking for...

The next day Bob had to fly to Las Vegas for work. I was curious about this arrangement. I then remembered that he was Jewish and everyone knows Jews love money. Of course there were going to be way more vaginas seeking immediate medical attention in Sin City than suburban Denver. I appreciated his sense of ambition. Bob was supposed to be gone for three days, but in an unexpected act of romance, Bob flew back home mid-cervical swab to see me for six hours.

Bob's efforts to court me made me feel so special and desired. I honestly just needed a pair of snow boots, a new reputable waxer, and I was ready to move to the Rocky Mountains. Bob took me to a few different stores before I decided on a pair of boots at Nordstrom. I followed the clerk up to the cash register and looked around, but Bob was nowhere to be found. I pulled out my credit card and quickly paid.

It wasn't that I necessarily expected Bob to buy my boots, although Hanukkah was right around the corner and it was his idea to take me boot shopping. It was more so the embarrassment I felt when it came time to pay and he had vanished. Starbucks must have been an anomaly; dude was definitely a Jew. I narrowed my eyes and prayed for a sudden chlamydia outbreak in Vegas to ensure he was summoned back to Sin City, stat.

After Bob left that evening, I calmed down. Maybe I had just misinterpreted the entire thing. People can be funny about money. Besides, there were more things I liked about him than not. The next night, my parents and I met up for a family meeting at a local burger joint. I told them I loved Colorado, had already found a kickass condo, and had met someone special. My enthusiasm was contagious as

I watched them become more excited about making the move.

A few days later, my parents and I returned to Orange County to pack our things. One morning, while I was buried in boxes, wondering if Denver was definitely meant to be my next home, Bob called to tell me he was on his way to see me. Clearly, this was a "sign" from the Universe that Denver was the right move. I deeply appreciated him for prioritizing me in his busy vagina schedule. I felt desired and his pursuit of me absolutely played into my deep attraction to men who go after what they want.

Bob drove from Vegas to Orange County. I was so excited to take him to all my favorite places, show him where I had grown up, and introduce him to my friends. I planned a lunch with my friends, Janet and Christoph, who invited us to their beautiful home in Newport Coast. They both liked Bob and we all had a lovely time together. As soon as Bob and I backed out of their driveway to head off onto the next adventure I had planned, Bob's mood had flipped entirely. He was cold and aloof. I tried to ask him what was wrong, but he was acting like such a condescending jerk, I just dropped it and turned up the music.

We drove down Pacific Coast Highway, where I intended for us to grab a cocktail overlooking the ocean. Unfortunately, Bob was still acting like he had chapped balls and someone had stolen his dog. Finally, I couldn't take it anymore and turned down the music to ask, "What is your problem?"

Bob launched into some story about how he had fallen in love with an Asian girl while he was in medical school and Janet had reminded him of her. He said the experience evoked memories of feeling unworthy and went on to explain that seeing the wealthy area where I am from made him question whether or not I was out of his league.

The shrink in me reassured him that everything was fine. I lavished him with compliments of his worthiness and thus began our pattern. Bob apologized for ruining what was meant to be a perfect day and drove back to Las Vegas. I made a special note never to take him to China Town in San Francisco. A large concentration of Asians like that could potentially render him incapacitated.

A few weeks later, Bob brought the twins out to California to visit before I moved. We were window shopping and stepped inside an old-fashioned candy shop. After thirty minutes, I started to get bored. I considered lighting up one of those candy cigarettes. Instead, I walked to the back of the store and started watching a movie they had on.

A few minutes later, I heard someone ask, "What about Stefanie?" I stood up and realized Bob and the kids were heading towards the door. I quickly walked over to them. I got to the door and instead of holding it open for me, Bob let the door close on my face. One of the girls noticed and quickly reopened the door for me. I said, "Wow. Thanks, Bob!" Bob acted as though he had no idea why I was upset. I told him he let the door shut on my face. Bob snarled, "Stop acting like a fucking princess, you're fine." Oh no, you did NOT just say that to me. Wasn't this the same dude who tried to show his daughters the importance of being treated well?

I got in the car, but I was so pissed I could not even look at him. Bob kept making snide comments. I finally snapped and told him to pull over so I could take an Uber. Bob refused to stop the car. The twins both started crying. I reached back and held their hands.

Bob launched into some long, senseless, boring-ass diatribe. He told the girls how relationships don't always work out and that they would be fine if we broke up. He said they might be sad for a little while, but they would get over it, blah, blah, blah. Puke.

We got back to the hotel where the four of us had been playing family. I walked in and packed up my things. I sat with each of the girls individually to calm them and let them know nothing was their fault. I made them repeat, "it is not my fault" back to me. As I was leaving the hotel room, Bob came in and asked if we could talk. I told him I was not comfortable discussing adult matters in front of his daughters. I reluctantly called my mom who came over to watch them while Bob and I went out to dinner to talk.

Bob poured his heart out to me. He told me he was scared to be so in love after being crushed by his divorce. He promised to go to therapy if I would still move to Colorado and stay with him. Bob's dad was a psychotherapist. I never met the guy, but obviously the old man had spent adequate time with his son because Bob had practically memorized all the psych lingo. Bob knew EXACTLY what to say to convince me that things would be different. He took accountability, apologized, and declared his commitment to change his behavior. I forgave him and we returned to the hotel.

On moving day, Bob agreed that if I would drive to Las Vegas, he would then drive the rest of the way to Colorado with me. I was nervous, but also excited to see where this new adventure would take me. Apparently, my first stop would be the doctors' lounge at the hospital where Bob worked. During his break, we started making out, but Bob couldn't get hard. It was sort of like dry humping a balloon animal. (I have never actually dry humped a balloon animal. Weird. This was just an example.)

Anyway, I tried everything I could think of and finally gave up. Bob became grumpy and short with me. I presume it was because his sexual dysfunction had embarrassed him. He decided now was the appropriate time to tell me that my online work bio was "too much" and needed to be edited down. When I told him that everything in my bio was true, he went on to say that I didn't need to name drop the universities I had attended. I found this more than peculiar, considering every doctor I know lists their schools' names, including him! After this nonsensical argument, Bob made arrangements for me to stay in a hotel on the strip. I checked into my room and cried alone the entire night. I deeply considered driving back to Orange County.

The next day, Bob picked me up as planned and we began our road trip to Denver. I could immediately tell that he had switched back to being in a good mood. This was divine intervention because there was no way I would have survived twelve hours in a car with the prick version of Bob. We drove through Utah and on into Colorado. Our goal was to get to Denver before dark.

By the time we got to a small mountain town two hours from Denver, I was absolutely famished. Bob offered to grab some snacks from the gas station, but I needed real food. We stopped at a Mexican restaurant and I promised to eat quickly.

We got back into the car only to find ourselves stuck in traffic. Bob immediately started yelling at me, "WE WOULDN'T BE LATE TO PICK UP MY KIDS FOR HANUKKAH IF YOU WEREN'T SO PICKY!" I felt so guilty, especially because it wasn't even good Mexican food. I wondered if he was this impatient with his patients when they were trying to push out human beings. "Listen, Nancy, I don't give a shit if it hurts! You should have thought about this before you had sex. I have a 3:30 tee time, and don't think I won't bill your ass if you make me late. NOW PUSH, BITCH!" I secretly laughed because I am hilarious.

We finally passed the accident that had caused the traffic and Bob proceeded to drive super fast down the winding mountain road, mocking me for being afraid when I asked him to slow down.

He kept making his usual passive aggressive comments until he got pulled over for driving like an asshole. We drove back in silence even though I totally wanted to scream, "I TOOOOOLD YOU SO, DUMMY." We picked up the kids, and everything was fine. Duh. Eye roll.

The next three months went by in a blur. I became increasingly close to his children. I spent almost every night at his house. I fell into a routine of taking care of the girls when he was in Las Vegas working. I helped them with homework, made lunches, cooked dinners, taught them to journal their feelings, took them to get their nails done...Basically, I was playing mom.

In these months, I also made excuses for Bob's blatant ungratefulness and frequent temper tantrums. I listened as he complained about how I loaded the dishwasher incorrectly and I how I had yet again, hung my purse on the back of a chair instead of in the closet. It began to occur to me that the reason he had never introduced me to any of his friends was because he did not have any. Bob was the kind of person to find fault in everyone and he had difficulty keeping his cool. All of his temper tantrums had occurred inside the home...until the day of the mall incident.

When his hissy fits went public, I knew this was the real Slim Shady and the man I had fallen for was a fraud. Bob was no longer able to maintain the nice guy facade. The truth is that although I was highly uncomfortable with his temperamental and outrageous behavior, I had begun to accept it.

During his first public tantrum, Toddler Bob became so enraged with one of his daughters that he smashed her phone in the middle of a mall food court. I promptly grabbed his other daughter's hand and we went for a walk around the upper level of the mall. All of this rage and poor excuse for discipline only to discover that Bob turned around and bought his daughter a brand new phone three days later. He didn't even take his own temper tantrums seriously. How could he expect his children to?

One day, Bob, the girls, and I went to Target to get them some summer clothes. I spent an hour in the dressing room with his daughters helping pick out several outfits. It was exhausting having to utilize my quasi-step-mom skills to insist they purchase clothes that actually covered their ass cheeks. When it came time to check out, I placed a toothbrush for myself on top of the pile of new clothes. Bob plucked it out and separated it so he wouldn't have to pay for it. Oh, so that's how you want to play? It's On, Motherfucker! I simply started dipping his toothbrush in the toilet while he was at work and abruptly stopped kissing him.

I also began reading books written by child psychologists so I could better learn to communicate with Bob on his childish level. My psych training was mostly with teens and adults. Because Bob's behavior more closely resembled a toddler, I needed to do some research. Would time-outs be effective for him? And if so, how long did he need to sit in the corner? Did I let him just cry it out? Some of the more helpful books I found included, but were not limited to: *The Defiant Child* and *The Survival Guide For Kids With Behavioral Challenges.*

My parents couldn't stand Bob and thought he had major mental issues. Their postulation was only strengthened when Bob invited me to go on his annual trip to Baltimore to meet his family for the first time. The night before we were scheduled to leave, I was at my condo packing. Bob called to discuss timing for arriving at the airport, and I asked him what I should pack. Bob became so insanely triggered, I glanced around wondering if he had spotted a random Asian. "I DON'T KNOW WHAT

YOU ARE SUPPOSED TO PACK! HAVEN'T YOU EVER PACKED YOUR OWN SUITCASE? WHY SHOULD I HAVE TO TELL YOU WHAT TO PACK?"

When I tried to explain to him that I simply didn't know what the itinerary was and wanted to be sure I was dressed appropriately, Bob kept verbally attacking me. I finally hung up the phone and took a few deep breaths before I sent a text to my mom. I told her what had just transpired and decided I was not going to go. Feeling empowered with her support of my decision, I called Bob back to inform him I would not be in attendance. Bob was absolutely furious.

He hung up on me and then promptly sent me a picture of my airline ticket to show me how much money he had lost. I cried myself to sleep. Just Kidding!!!! I drank a couple glasses of Prisoner wine and binge watched "Bachelor in Paradise."

I began distancing myself from Bob and started staying at my condo. I realized that I had become so engrossed in Bob and his children that I had not met any friends in my new city. I didn't even know what I was doing in Colorado. In a moment of weakness, I called him sobbing. I was having a hard time catching my breath, I was nauseas, and my heart was racing. I had never experienced anything like this before and I seriously thought I was having a heart attack.

Bob and the girls came over and took me to the emergency room. The doctors ran a series of tests and informed me I was having a panic attack. Bob complained the entire time about how late it was and how I was keeping him up. Wait. You are pissed I am not having a heart attack? That's totally psycho. I decided I was going to yelp review his psychotherapist dad: Job not well done, sir.

I vowed not to return to Bob after this. He repeatedly called, begging me to come back. He showed up with flowers. He said all the right things. I desperately missed the kids. And once again, I decided to give him another chance. It's so obvious to me now that Bob knew exactly what I needed to hear, as most verbal abusers do.

As a way to sort of re-set our relationship, Bob invited me to go to the mountains with him and the girls. After we spent the day zip-lining, I helped the kids get ready for dinner that night and was the last one to shower. I could tell Bob was agitated that I wasn't ready to go. I desperately tried to recall what the child psychology books said about warding off an impending tantrum. Shit. Too late. Bob rudely announced that he and the kids would be waiting in the lobby and for me to hurry up.

After hurrying to get dressed and made up, I walked downstairs and watched as he angrily strode across the parking lot. I felt something shift inside me. This was NOT going to be my reality. I wanted to be with someone that was uplifting and fun, someone who made life happier and gentler. I hugged the twins and then leaned over the driver's side window and said, "You girls go and have a special time with your dad!" The twins immediately began to protest. Bob barked, "I can't believe you're not coming!" He then put the car in reverse without waiting for me to move and almost ran over my foot.

A sense of unrelenting strength suddenly flooded through me. Alone, I went and ate at a fancy wine bistro next to the hotel. After my second glass of cabernet, I made the decision that this relationship was officially over. I would no longer allow myself to be treated this way. Since an Uber was going to cost around a thousand bucks, I decided to buy a train ticket. The next available departure was at 7 am the next morning.

I sighed and shrugged. Anyone who knows me, knoooows I am not messing around if I am getting up at that godforsaken hour. When women (and gay men) ask me how I keep my skin looking flawless, I be sure to let them in on nature's best-kept secret: sleep til noon. Seriously, my skin has never been exposed to sun. I am entirely nocturnal. I did decide, however, to make an exception to escape this vacation with the "Fun Police."

Later that night, I let myself back into the hotel room. Bob was sleeping on the couch. I gathered my things, kissed his daughters on the forehead, and tried to catch a few winks before sunrise. I softly closed the door behind me and we never spoke again. I have never met a more manipulative, neurotic, mean, angry, vindictive, spiteful, narcissistic, condescending, erratic person. I also feel tremendous empathy for anyone who lives such a tortured existence.

"I fucking tried to love you, but you don't know how to love."
—Me (But pretend this is in Italian.)

Toddler Bob—not my person.

Take It From Me...
- Never, ever tolerate being in an abusive relationship.
- Pay attention to ALL the red flags.
- Do not involve children in adult matters.
- Most people who think you are "too much" are the same people who feel like they are "not enough."
- Never be with someone that nobody likes.
- Train rides from the mountains are actually beautiful.

El Diablo Bob

I know you're getting tired of hearing this, but I met El Diablo Bob...online. After being with Toddler Bob, who was such a downer, I was not looking for anything serious. El Diablo Bob and I met for lunch with the agreement that we were just going to be "friends" since he had recently become single as well. I told him the truth about being a doctor, an actress, and all the things I have accomplished that typically emasculate most men. Bob remained undeterred. I learned he was divorced with a four-year-old son and owned a couple tire shops. Bob was funny and super attractive in a ripped, Mexican hipster, Vin Diesel way. We ended up staying and talking for three hours. My head tilted. Hmmm...Maybe I was looking for something more serious after all.

I finally told Bob I had to go since I had recently purchased another investment property and needed to go set up the Wi-Fi before my renters moved in. Bob offered to come help me. My parents happened to be there placing finishing touches on the place, so I decided Bob could also meet my family on day numero uno. (I was already beginning to speak his native dialect.) I had dated some real characters and thought Mom and Dad could be a new addition to my initial screening process with my gentlemen callers.

My parents were polite, but it was obvious they were not immediate fans of Bob. I was a little surprised that my parents acted so standoffish towards him since he was seemingly such a nice person. In fact, I think the only thing they liked about him was that he could set up Wi-Fi passwords, and even this isn't an altogether challenging task when one lives in a major metropolitan city. I threw caution to the wind. I wanted something light-hearted and easy.

Bob was FUN. He treated life like a game that we could play, and every day was a new adventure. This was a stark contrast to the nightmare I lived for five months with Toddler Bob. Right away, we began spending every day together. We were both business owners and took full advantage of our flexible schedules.

We spent the next few days exploring Denver since I had only been living here a year and the first five months were spent being cooped up with Toddler Bob. El Diablo Bob showed me all over the town. We would ride his scooter to his favorite hot spots and walk through the Arts District to check out the latest local artists. We really should have purchased stock in Uber at the rate we were using them to bar hop. Bob was like having my own personal, extremely attractive tour guide.

I learned Bob had some dough and, being the self-proclaimed philanthropist I am, I happily helped him spend it on me. Bob spoiled me with delicious food at Zagat-Rated restaurants, spa treatments, professions of adoration, and amazing sex. His muscles, olive skin, generosity, and zest for life were positively intoxicating. Being with him was like the highest of highs.

Four days after we met, Bob and I flew to Tucson to escape the cold and so he could introduce me to his Mamí and Papí. I definitely liked Bob, but I loooooooved his family. They were some of the sweetest, most welcoming people I had ever met. To this day, I have yet to find enchiladas that compare to Mamí's.

The day we returned from our weekend getaway, Bob gave me a key to his house. We had known each other for seven days. He said I was welcome to come over and stay any time. He told me to treat his home like my own and that he wanted me to know I could completely trust him. My toothbrush, some miscellaneous items, and my vagina promptly moved themselves right on in.

Two weeks later, we decided to fly back down to Tucson to see his parents again. The night before we left on our trip, I decided to put him through another screening process since all of this was happening so fast. I met up with one of his ex-girlfriends whom he had been with for four years. Karla absolutely raved about Bob. She told me she had "not seen him this happy in years." She went on and on about how thrilled she was for us. Bob received the full green light from his ex. OMG. Maybe this was real!!!!! We left for Arizona. I felt incredible.

Mamí and Papí were so excited to see me again. It was rare to meet people who shared my enthusiasm for traditional family values. I could just see these people teaching their future Mexican-Jewish grandchildren how to make tamales while Bob was out replacing the tires of a G-Class Mercedes on the driveway. I wondered if our little Mexican kids would be into futbol (or what you uncultured Americans refer to as "soccer") or baseball. I figured we would be able to determine their natural talents when they broke their birthday pinatas using either their feet or their bats.

That evening the four of us went out to dinner. His parents were positively glowing with pride. They were obviously ecstatic that their first-generation American son had an attractive, blonde doctor on his arm. At one point, Bob asked a passerby to take a picture of the four of us and posted it online with the caption: "People I love the most in the world." Almost immediately, his phone started blowing up. I smiled naively thinking that it was all of his friends congratulating him on finding his soulmate. I couldn't have been more wrong.

A few minutes after Bob posted the picture, he inexplicably became agitated and cold towards me. We returned to his parent's house and he insisted on sleeping in the other room. WTF? I couldn't figure out what was happening. It was literally like night and day. He was acting like such a blatant asshole that his parents apologized for his behavior. I told Bob I wanted to go home and asked him to please take me to the airport. We began driving, but he apologized and convinced me to stay until the following day when we were scheduled to leave together.

We went out a few more times after we returned to Denver, but nothing was quite the same after Arizona. One night, when I told Bob I was going out to celebrate my belated birthday with my friend Kathy, Bob begged me to stay at his place to "hang out and watch movies." I sweetly declined, told him I would be back in a few hours, kissed him, and left. A little while later, I sent him a picture of me blowing out my candles. Bob responded with, "Happy Birthday" and nothing else. I felt my head slowly drifting to the right in yet, another tilt. I shrugged it off, told myself to enjoy the present moment with one of my best girl friends, and did exactly that.

On my way home, I called Bob. He didn't answer. I sent multiple texts. He never responded. Something was definitely up because I could not shake the uncomfortable gnawing feeling I had in my stomach. Ordinarily, my neurotic Jewish worry would kick in and I would be wondering if he had been in a car accident, had gotten shot, nicked an artery while cutting an apple, had fallen on the floor and was lying there with all of his limbs broken, unable to reach the phone with his tongue, or had even...died.

In any other situation, I would have driven to his house to see if he was okay, but this was a different kind of "something is wrong." My gut knew he was not flopping around on his floor like a fish.

I left Bob one final voicemail that night and then went home to sleep. I tossed and turned most of the night. The next day, while trolling through his social media page, I saw he had been active within the hour. I repeatedly called and texted him, to no avail. This went on for several more days and into the weekend.

As the week passed, my confusion and frustration grew. Why was I being ghosted? I truly could not figure out what I had done to deserve being treated this way. How could someone be so into me, beg me to stay with him the last time I was with him, and then suddenly do an emotionless about face and go M.I.A.?

Weeks went by, and slowly my friends and family helped me see how odd the entire situation was from the beginning. I realized I had been so in love with the idea of being in love that I had overlooked some entirely brazen red flags. I realized that while playing, laughter, great chemistry, and a fun orientation to life are must-haves, Bob was too reckless for me with his partying, throwing money around, and lack of involvement with his son. I wanted to find a healthy balance. I wanted to be with someone who had stability AND a playful personality. Besides, everything had happened way too fast. It had been an utter whirlwind, and I had allowed myself to get swept away.

I had just reached a place of acceptance for another failed relationship, when I received a random phone call from a woman named Raquel. She claimed to be Bob's ex-girlfriend. Again, I felt my head tilt.

Raquel informed me that she had been with Bob for two years and that he was a total scumbag. She said Bob was a manipulative liar, a deadbeat dad, and that she wanted nothing to do with him. She said she was even strongly considering filing a restraining order against him because he would not leave her alone. She told me that he had been texting her the night we were in Arizona and he had posted that picture. It was Raquel who had been blowing up his phone. Apparently, El Diablo Bob had been trying to win her back the entire time I was dating him and when she saw the photo he posted of us with his parents, she completely lost her shit.

Raquel went on to inform me that Bob had domestic violence charges filed against him by his ex-wife and this was the real reason he never saw his son. She also said that when he had stopped all contact with me, it was because he had flown down to Texas to be with her. She knew all about my egg freezing consultation because he had accompanied me to my appointment, apparently to gather information for her. Raquel warned me to be careful with him. I felt sick. I knew she was telling me the truth.

Raquel informed me that she was coming back to Colorado the following week since she had things she wanted to get back from Bob's house. We made arrangements to meet and instantly hit it off. At the very least, Bob had exquisite taste in women.

We decided to go to Bob's house together to retrieve our possessions. Fortunately, I was smart enough to grab my vagina when I left to go out that fateful night for my birthday, but I still had a necklace and an expensive pair of boots over there. We decided to call the police to have an officer escort us since we knew Bob was probably going to lose his damn mind.

We pulled up to Bob's house with a police officer and rang the bell. Bob opened the door and instantly paled as his brain fumbled to make sense of the situation. He looked as though he had seen two ghosts. He immediately began begging Raquel to take him back. He. Was. Hysterical. The officer told him to calm down and let us retrieve our belongings. Bob continued to manically rant, vacillating between calling me horrible names and repeatedly apologizing to Raquel.

Raquel grabbed everything she could. Unfortunately, my stuff was nowhere to be found. We walked out the front door, got into her car, and started laughing in disbelief. Within minutes, Raquel's phone started blowing up with texts and calls from Bob. Each time, she sent him straight to voicemail, refusing to answer him.

We called Papí on speaker phone from Raquel's car to let him know what had just transpired. In his thick accent, Papí told us to stay away from his son. He then told us he often didn't like Bob and warned us to be careful. I realized Papí had probably been filled with a false sense of optimism that his son was finally turning his pathetic life around when he had brought me home. I still have no idea how such beautiful human beings were able to spawn the mother-fucking devil himself.

Traditionally, Jews don't believe in Satan, but considering I had actually met him in person, I am confident I could present a compelling argument as an addendum to the Torah. It was like one of Mamí's rogue eggs was fertilized by one of Papí's demon seed and El Diablo Bob was spit out into the Universe. My head tilted for the millionth time since I met this man. I decided to make an appointment with my chiropractor as soon as we got off the phone with Papí.

After this, Raquel and I would check in with each other every other month or so. About three months after we had gone to Bob's house together, Raquel called to tell me that Bob had broken into her house and beat her within an inch of her life. I was positively horrified knowing this had happened to this poor woman and also faced with the harsh reality that this easily could have been me. Raquel pressed charges and Bob went to jail.

I recently saw Bob while I was out with friends in Denver. We never acknowledged each other, and I can't be sure that he saw me. I was absolutely paralyzed with fear by the sight of him. My body trembled uncontrollably and my breathing became labored as I recalled the trauma that had ensued from our chance encounter only two years prior. My friends and I left and I never looked back.

El Diablo Bob—not my person.

Take It From Me...

- You do not make friends on dating websites.
- It's okay to move at any pace in a relationship, as long as that pace allows you to stay in touch with reality enough to see red flags.
- Sociopaths will stop at nothing to get what they want.
- Mind control and manipulation tactics (ie: giving you a house key, introducing you to family prematurely, taking instant vacations) can trick your mind into thinking the relationship is further along than it really is.
- People who try that hard to prove you can trust them (ie: giving you a house key on day seven of knowing you) usually have something to hide.
- There is no Mexican food on earth that is worth dying over.

Fertility Bob

After Toddler Bob and El Diablo Bob, my faith tank was running low. I was really beginning to doubt that Colorado was the home of my future husband. But, the second I laid eyes on Fertility Bob, I could feel my ovaries pulsating. I stared at this fine specimen sitting at the bar waiting for me…6'2, sandy blonde hair, chiseled face, golden tan, bright blue eyes, expensive suit, divorced. He looked like the adult version of my childhood boyfriend, Cheetah Bob. *Please don't be a fucking moron, please don't be a fucking moron*, I chanted silently. *Or if you are a fucking moron, at least don't have a small penis.* I took a deep breath, smoothed my little black dress, and strode forward to meet the future father of my children.

Our chemistry was palpable, the conversation flowed, he laughed at my jokes, and chewed with his mouth closed. We kissed a few times and it was perfect. God, there is nothing like a great kisser. His vernacular did not include the words "hot" or "big jugs," and he was viably employed by…wait for it…waaaaaait for it…A FERTILITY COMPANY. This man was a literal baby maker. No joke, that morning, I had JUST finished my final pre-cycle appointment with my fertility doctor to have my eggs frozen! I was so enamored by him that I immediately shushed my brain when she began to question Fertility Bob's motives behind requesting to eat at the bar rather than a table.

A couple hours later, I realized the restaurant was emptying. We had closed the place down. In my naiveté, I believed this was due to my captivating presence and to the obvious fact that we were falling in love. In reality, Fertility Bob had become so drunk that he had rendered himself immobile. He made a valiant attempt to stand only to realize his massive stature was an unworthy opponent to gravity. The bartender, restaurant manager, and I somehow wrestled him outside to his Uber.

I watched as my now future ex-husband slumped over and crawled into the 1997 Mazda Miata. I mouthed "It's our first date" and gave a thumbs up to the restaurant staff. They laughed, but the pity they felt for me was written all over their faces. Being the Good Samaritan that I am, I reluctantly climbed in after his ass because he had conveniently forgotten where he lived. Though he outweighed me by a hundred pounds, I somehow felt it was my duty to ensure he arrived home safely.

In a brief moment of clarity, Fertility Bob nobly managed to tell the driver the name of the street he lived on, but could not remember which mansion was his. He also graciously divulged that he no longer had a driver's license due to "a couple DUI's." I nodded in solidarity with the judicial system's decision pertaining to this matter.

As we turned onto his street, Fertility Bob mumbled for the Uber driver to "just let him out." The driver looked back at me, seeking some sort of approval, and I just rolled my eyes. He pulled over and Fertility Bob opened the door, flopped out, and rolled onto someone's lawn with an audible groan. The Uber driver and I stood there for a second, until he broke the silence with, "I think you should just leave him…"

I bit my lip, "I can't just leave him on a lawn!"

"Why not? It's a nice neighborhood and it's summer. He'll be fine."

"Yeah, but what if he dies? We would be accessories to a death or something. Look at me! I would never survive prison! Those women would devour me."

More silence.

Finally I said, "Just go. I will be fine."

The Uber driver shrugged and drove off.

I sat down on the curb next to Fertility Bob, "Bob! Hey Bob, so, do any of these houses look vaguely familiar? Like maybe one you might have raised your first family in? Think birthdays, holidays, swing-sets, maybe your first DUI?" I laughed at my joke and poked his gigantic leg with my finger. He groaned again and his cell phone fell out of his pocket.

He had mentioned his son frequently throughout dinner, so I picked up his cell phone and scrolled through his contacts until I found someone with his name. I called the number while examining my cuticles, "Hello?" croaked a sleepy voice on the other end. "Hi there, buddy! So, my name is Stefanie and I am out with your Dad and he is ummm…not feeling well."

"Oh God, not again. Where is he?"

I looked over at Fertility Bob, "Well, you should know he is alive…It is just that he is outside sleeping on a lawn, but I think we might be on your street! Could you maybe tell me your address?"

"Hang on. I will be right down."

A minute later, a light came on in a house a couple doors

down. Good call on the street, Fertility Bob! I picked up his giant limp arm, gave him a high-five, and let it flop back to the ground. I then waved at the gangly kid who looked to be about nineteen jogging towards us. Just then Fertility Bob started moaning and fumbling with his zipper. I shrieked, "OH GOD! HE'S PEEING!"

"DAD, NO!"

Too late...I watched in horrified bewilderment as Fertility Bob somehow managed to hoist his gargantuan mass of dead weight onto his side, free his junk, and piss on his neighbor's perfectly manicured front yard. I looked over at his mortified son and told him, "Honestly, it's no big deal, let's just get him home." Only it was kind of a "big deal" because we had to actually get the beast home.

We somehow managed to wrestle Fertility Bob into the house. I called another Uber and sat down on the couch to wait. His son came downstairs and sat with me, apologizing profusely for his dad's behavior. He even graciously offered to drive me home in his dad's former Porsche. I felt so sad as I glanced around at what would appear to an outsider to be a perfect home and wondered where it all went wrong.

I didn't have much time to ponder this because right then someone started pounding on the front door. The kid stood up just as some lady burst through and marched straight on upstairs screaming at Fertility Bob. I figured the evening wasn't a total loss, considering I had now met my target heart rate multiple times. I definitely was not going to the gym in the morning.

The tiny blonde tornado came whipping back down the stairs and yelled, "If your dad can't get his shit together, I am DONE." Even if I wasn't a trained psychologist, I could garner this would not be happening anytime soon. And why are you threatening his kid?

This situation would pay my mortgage for years if I was treating these people.

Fortunately, the broad assumed I was on a date with Fertility Bob's son or she probably would have tried to murder me right then. I was so tired from lugging Bob around Denver, that she might have actually succeeded. My Uber arrived and I said goodbye to Fertility Bob's son.

The next morning, I woke up and realized I had broken my Louboutin heel during the fiasco. This was the final straw. I rattled off a text to Fertility Bob telling him, "I want to be compensated for the damage you caused my designer heel." And to me for ruining my evening. And to your sweet son who did not need to be cleaning up his father's messes. And also, to that little angry woman.

Fertility Bob appeared to be embarrassed by his actions. Due to his brief-form letter apology, I realized he was familiar with such remorse. He left me $300 cash in an adorable decorative bird's nest on his front porch, and I never spoke to him again.

Fertility Bob—not my person.

Take It From Me...

- Do not sit at the bar for a dinner date.
- Make sure your date is ambulatory. *Wheelchairs excluded.
- Request to see a valid driver's license.
- Do not EVER, EVER settle for someone who isn't willing to give you what you are worth.
- Be brave enough to walk away; your spirit knows what she is doing.

Bub

Not surprisingly, I met my current boyfriend online. Bub (not Bob) and I exchanged a few messages before I left on a trip to Israel with my mom. I was hosting a charity event when I got home and decided to invite him. He didn't come that night, but he thanked me for inviting him and did ask for my number. A couple days later, he called and asked me out.

Actually, his exact words were, "Do you want to go on a date or what?" My knees went weak. Just kidding. I rolled my eyes and thought, "Here we go again..." I agreed and Bub suggested we go bowling. Bowling? Strike two. Pun intended. I hesitated for a second before giving him a resounding, "Um sure..."

It was snowing out, and I arrived at the bowling alley before him. I turned around and this time my knees really did go weak. Holy shit. This guy was so hot. He was tall, with a gorgeous smile and beautiful blue eyes. We had a cocktail and then went bowling. Bub asked if I needed an extra pair of socks. I looked at him inquisitively. He said, "You know, so you have clean socks when you put your own shoes back on. Anyway, I brought you some." He handed me a pair of socks. A part of my heart melted at his thoughtful gesture.

I jokingly asked, "Are you an Aquarius? This is totally something I would do!"

Bub looked at me curiously and said, "I actually am."

"When's your birthday?" I asked him. Bub told me it was February 1st, and I promptly dropped my bowling shoes and my new loaner socks. "My birthday is February 1st too." We both started laughing and got super excited.

Bub and I decided to have a little contest while bowling. I told him if I won, I wanted a ninety-minute massage by a real masseuse. He said if he won, he got a second date. He kicked my ass, but graciously took me to go get a couple's massage on our second date. After our massages, we sat in the car talking.

Bub opened up and told me about all the skeletons in his closet. (I mean this figuratively. If he had actual dead people in his closet, I would have called it right then.) The dude put it all out on the line. He told me about his divorce and how he had been addicted to drugs twenty years prior. He told me he suffered from clinical depression at times. I didn't necessarily like what I was hearing, but I deeply appreciated his honesty. It was different and strangely refreshing. He looked at me and asked if I was still interested in dating him. I slowly nodded.

Fast forward two years. Bub and I are still together. Actually, we moved in together after our third date. I typically don't recommend expedited co-habitation, but for some reason, this felt right. Bub meets all my checklist requirements (aside from not being Jewish). He is smart, kind, generous, creative, good looking, attentive, protective, loyal, honest, moral, folds laundry neurotically well, and he is my best friend. Oh, and he makes a mean cup of coffee.

Bub and I love, laugh, and play hard together. We have traveled, celebrated holidays, met one another's families and friends (my parents and friends adore him), and we have recently started a business together. I knew I was all in when I didn't mind giving him suppositories every morning for a week, when desperate measures called. Essentially, we met and it was game on.

Now, it definitely hasn't been all sunshine and roses. Bub and I have had some monumental disagreements (all of which are clearly his fault, since I am obviously perfect) and we can fight like the best of them. The difference is we are both deeply committed to changing the belief systems that are no longer serving us in this life. And this means doing the scary, hard work of leaning into and examining our wounds and triggers.

I feel scared when his depression surfaces and he pushes me away. I instinctively become curt and insensitive, since one of my deepest wounds is feeling left out. I can tell when Bub lets his old programs of feeling unworthy take over. I watch from a place of compassionate detachment when he goes into panic mode. I feel his pain as he rages and cries out, questioning if he is good enough for me. But as time goes on and we keep doing the work, we become better people and partners.

Bub is introspective and deeply intuitive. He is a stark contrast to the men I dated before. He's not intimidated by me. He doesn't try to control or compete with me. He is proud of me. He is always there when I need him to catch me, and I am there to catch him. He is crazy enough to love the things about me that I am most insecure about. And that alone has healed some deep hurts I have carried around for far too long.

Because of Bub, I can look at old pictures from my chubby days and laugh instead of wanting to crawl in a hole and die from embarrassment. In this relationship, I have finally freed myself of twenty-five years of eating disorders and body dysmorphia. I have learned to be okay with uncomfortable emotions and being triggered. Now, instead of shutting down, hitting below the belt, or giving up...I stay, dig in, and find the gift in the pain. And there are so many gifts.

For the first time in my life, I have finally experienced what it feels like to have a soulful partner who deeply believes in me and loves me for exactly who I am. I feel seen, understood, and absolutely adored. The deep love I feel from Bub is on par with the love I have always felt from my parents. With him in my life, I feel like I can do anything. My soul feels at ease and my heart feels safe. And we laugh...oh boy, do we laugh. Sometimes I think we are both eternally eight years old.

Because Bub is so vulnerable with me, I can finally be vulnerable the way I always dreamed of, but never thought possible. We have formed a conscious partnership and are helping each other heal from past hurts so that we can be truly free from the shackles of old, crippling belief systems. And for the first time in my life, my perspective has completely shifted from desperately seeking a happy ending to enjoying the actual experience of each day.

Bub—the perfect person for me right now and maybe forever.

Take It From Me...
- Don't ever settle.
- Forget the outcome and focus on the growth.
- Find a partner that is equally invested and committed to self-work.
- Do not make yourself small to appease others.
- You are lovable.
- You are worthy.
- Sometimes agreeing to go bowling can change your life.

Conclusion

When I set out to write this book, I thought it would be a fun little adventure where I would talk about all the Bobs it took for me to get to my Bub. All the funny, outlandish stories that my married friends have enjoyed hearing over the years. Boy, was I in for a surprise! Turns out that writing this book has been more like a complete soul striptease where I am standing in front of the entire world with my pants around my ankles. This process has required tremendous courage and admittedly, a few cases of red wine. Little did I know that this journey would also come complete with its very own paradigm shift.

There were moments when I wanted to quit writing. I was embarrassed of my choices, afraid of judgment, worried what others would think, and exhausted from reliving the trauma of some of my past relationships. Thank God I had Bub's support and encouragement to keep going, despite his discomfort in my traveling down memory lane with all the men who came before him. And I cannot even begin to express the appreciation I have for the best writing partner in the world, Erin. She would continually remind me why we set out to do this and how many people we would be able to help with the humor and the heartache. So here I am, at the end of my book, with my big girl pants on (not around my ankles), overcoming my impulse to hide or play small.

No longer am I the girl with laser focus on the outcome. No longer do I forecast my relationship. I am now fully in the present moment and entirely devoted to growth and enjoying the journey. I used to be the girl that would go on a kick ass first date and on my way home, daydream about our wedding. And if he was a great kisser, my imagination would go into overdrive, conjuring up visual images of what our kids would look like. Seriously, after one date! I was unwavering in my focus on the outcome, on the happy ending (not that kind, pervs).

The scary part of forecasting, other than setting myself up for disappointment time and again, is that I would also trick my subconscious into thinking we were further along in our relationship than we really were. You see, the subconscious does not know the difference between real and imaginary. So when I would create these vivid little home movies in my head detailing my future with Bob-whoever, my mind thought this was actually happening. So, when I would show up on date #2, I had already walked down the aisle with the dude across from me, who in reality didn't even know my middle name. I can only imagine that I came across a bit too comfortable, too familiar.

I am sure this was simultaneously reassuring for the man I was dating and also quite confusing. The narcissistically-inclined Bobs probably thought they had it in the bag; while the decent-minded Bobs knew they had not earned my being so comfortable with them. I am certain that I made it too easy for some and too intimate for others. Dang, have I learned a lot! I do give myself some slack, though. After all, we are a society heavily programmed to achieve, accomplish, and create results. And full disclosure, this has worked for me in just about every other area of my life.

At forty, I have now learned that love works differently. Love is not formulaic, there is no paint-by-number recipe to follow. It is very much an alive, dynamic, and ever-changing beast all its own. This hard-learned and hard-earned lesson has me both terrified and excited. It is terrifying to know that I do not have full control over it. It is exciting because boredom will never take up residence in my relationship. With heart wide open, I welcome the surprises and even the triggers. I know and trust that everything is working out the way it is meant to work out. The triggers come up as gifts for me to get honest with myself, heal, and grow. And as the Aquarius who craves change and challenge, this is actually quite ideal.

Even though I couldn't always see it at the time, every relationship I have entered into has taught me something about myself. The truth is, each relationship was a gift and none of them were "mistakes." Each experience reflected back to me the areas where I needed to grow so that I could continue to evolve into the best version of myself. It was all part of the plan the entire time. When I stand back to look at the tapestry of my life, I can see just how beautifully it has been woven together.

I have become a better friend, daughter, doctor, coach, actress, and human being because of the people I have encountered along my way. I have such profound appreciation for all that I have experienced because I know every last bit of it was necessary. Each relationship helped me to become more aligned with the things I must have in a partnership. Even more importantly, I have learned my true sense of self-worth was never derived from my physical appearance, my intelligence, money, or the titles behind my name. I am proud of everything I have accomplished, but I also know this is not where my power lies.

I have reached a place of contentment and peace in knowing that right now, I am exactly who I am supposed to be. The line has been drawn, and I finally have the clarity I so desperately sought. I have learned to love, trust, and forgive the person who has been with me throughout this entire journey...myself.

Other Publications

She: Poems
Erin-Says.com
www.KeepItSimpleSilly.net

Other Products Services

Eden Experiences www.edenexperiences.com
Beloved Rebel Media www.belovedrebelmedia.com

Stefanie Biography

Stefanie Bernritter Kleine was born and raised in Orange County, California. Graduating high school at 16, she went on to earn her Master's and Ph.D. in Psychology. At a young age, Stefanie knew she was driven by two impulses: to create and to inspire. Her creativity led her to film and TV acting as well as publishing her first book, *She: Poems*, at the age of 26. Driven by a deep desire to inspire others, Stefanie opened a private practice as a Life and Business Coach 16 years ago. Over the past year, she has built a healing and wellness retreat center in Colorado as well as founding Beloved Rebel Media. Stefanie feels endlessly blessed as she has created a life that feeds both her creativity and her passion to help others live their best lives possible. Stefanie lives with her boyfriend, Bub, just outside of Denver, Colorado.

Erin Biography

Erin Moroni is an author and creator of the blog, erin-says.com. She is a founding partner in Beloved Rebel Media. With a degree from Colorado State University, Erin has been writing for over ten years. She has three children, a husband, and a large extended family who consistently provide her with a wide array of comedic material. In her spare-time she enjoys spending time with her children when they are not being punks, adopting dogs with issues, and arguing with her husband about the number of dogs with issues she has adopted. She currently lives with her family in Colorado.